AVALANCHE
SAFETY

FOR SKIERS & CLIMBERS

SECOND EDITION

TONY DAFFERN

THE
MOUNTAINEERS

Published by
The Mountaineers
1001 SW Klickitat Way, Suite 201
Seattle, WA 98134

Simultaneously published in Canada by
Rocky Mountain Books, Calgary

Simultaneously published in the United
Kingdom by Diadem Books, London

Printed and bound in Canada by Jasper
Printing Group Ltd. Edmonton

Front cover photo: *Ice avalanche in the
Canadian Rockies. The skiers are travelling a
popular route to the Bow Hut on the Wapta
Icefields.* Photo by Kevin Cronin.

Cover design by Jennifer Shontz

ISBN 0-89886-647-2

Acknowledgments

A book of this nature relies heavily on the knowledge, research and writing of others. This book is an
attempt to organize and condense a vast amount of
information normally available only to the snow
science community or to professional mountain
guides, and to interpret this information in light of
my experience as a backcountry skier and climber. I
have resisted the suggestion that every quote or
source should be cited in referenced footnotes. There
is a bibliography on page 184 and a list of major
references on page 189 for those of you who wish to
read further on the subject.

However, I would like to thank several people
who have made a major contribution to backcountry
avalanche safety and whose work has had considerable influence on the presentation of material in
this book.

Special thanks are due to Doug Fesler of Anchorage,
Alaska, for permission to reproduce a major portion
of his paper on Choosing a Safe Route and Decision
Making used in Chapter 8, and to the National
Research Council of Canada, under the leadership
of Peter Schaerer who, in conjunction with the British
Columbia Institute of Technology, developed the
material on the Shovel Shear Test and snow pit
observations used in Chapter 5 and the rationale for
hazard evaluation used in Chapter 7.

I would also like to acknowledge the contribution to backcountry avalanche safety made by Bruce
Tremper and Brad Meiklejohn as a result of their
addressing the issue of stability evaluation for the
backcountry skier and for promoting safe skiing.

Thanks also to Dale Gallagher for his help and
encouragement, to Mrs. Martha Atwater for permission to reproduce the extract from Monty Atwater's
book "The Avalanche Hunters" on page 160, to
Hodder & Stoughton for the quotation from Chris
Bonington's book "Everest—South West Face", and
to Pete Martinelli for permission to use material from
the "Avalanche Handbook".

There were many people who assisted me in vari-
ous ways. I hope this list is complete and apologize
if I have missed anyone. Thanks to Dr. Eizi Akitaya,
Tim Auger, Don Beers, Steve Couche, Greg Crawford,
Kevin Cronin, Tom Davidson, Jim Davies, Roland
Emetaz, Bruno Engler, George Field, Peter Furhman,
Dr. F. Furukawa, Dale Gallagher, Lloyd Gallagher,
Frank Grover, Claire Israelson, Bruce Jamieson, Seiiti
Kinosita, Leon Kubbernus, Nick Logan, Rudolf
Ludwig, Hamish MacInnes, Brad Meiklejohn, Kris
Newman, Andy Nicol, Ron Perla, André Roche, Steve
Rothfels, Tony Salway, Bob Sandford, Al Schaffer,
Alf Skrastins, Chris Stethem, Lars Suneby, Rod Ward
and Knox Williams.

Contents

Fig, 1 A slab avalanche in prime telemarking
terrain at the head of Little Yoho Valley, Yoho
National Park. Photo Rudi Setz Collection.

"We should condemn men for crossing snow slopes in a condition favorable to avalanches, as we should condemn them for indulging in a cruise in an unseaworthy ship."

Leslie Stephen, 1865

Foreword

The 21st and 22nd of February 1981 was not a good weekend to go ski touring in the Canadian Rockies. A long spell of cold clear weather at the beginning of the month had given way to a series of storms coming in from the west. Across the Columbia Trench, in the Purcells, 180 cm of snow had fallen in the previous ten days. Farther east in the Rockies, more moderate snowfalls accompanied by strong winds had created treacherous pockets of wind slab on all lee slopes. Surface hoar produced by the cold spell was now sandwiched like a loose filling of feathery crystals 45 cm below the new snow surface. As the weekend approached, snowfall became light to intermittent and the temperature rose to a relatively mild -5°C during the warmest part of the day. Slopes were now in prime condition to slide; all they needed was a trigger.

It was Saturday around noon. Four experienced ski tourers traversing the Wapta Icefields became concerned about the increasing hazard and rather than carry out their planned route decided to abort down the Des Poilus Glacier and Waterfall Valley to Yoho Valley. Bad routefinding led them into a narrow ravine only a few kilometres from the top of Twin Falls. The first man had just made it safely through when he heard a swooshing noise behind him and on looking round saw the second skier being pushed down into the creek by a small slab avalanche and buried under 8 metres of snow. A rescue beacon search revealed nothing, despite the digging of a huge pit in an effort to reduce the tremendous depth of snow between themselves and the victim. Probing with short ski poles proved equally useless in the circumstances. It was a long way to the nearest road and the cry for help wasn't received until 10:00 that night. On Sunday, around 10:30 am, the National Parks Rescue Group, using fine probing, located the body lying face-down in the creek; he had been pinned down by the weight of snow and drowned.

While the recovery operation was going on, the mountains were busy claiming two more victims. Thirteen kilometres away across the same icefields, three climbers were attempting to climb Mount Thompson on skis. All three were relatively inexperienced in winter mountaineering and certainly knew nothing about the danger from avalanches or they would never have chosen the route they did. They had read the high hazard warning at the Banff warden's office when they picked their hut permit but didn't take it seriously. So there they were starting up a steep bowl in the centre of the face. At the last minute, the third man decided it was easier and quicker to scramble up the rock ridge to one side and wait for his companions above the bowl. When they didn't turn up he climbed up and down the ridge a bit thinking they had either gone on ahead or had decided to follow his route after all. Still nothing. He then descended the bowl and was lucky to be caught by only a small avalanche which gave him a ride to the bottom of the slope. After extracting himself, he noticed that there were other slides about, but not realizing their significance returned to the hut feeling sure he would find his friends waiting. Of course they weren't there either and he must have spent many anxious wondering hours before rushing off to get help.

That same afternoon, many kilometres nearer to Banff, four cross-country skiers had finally made it up the long steep trail to Bourgeau Lake. After lunch the two women returned to the car while the men carried on beyond the lake towards a small pass. Although the first skier was carrying a shovel, they seemed unaware of the high avalanche hazard and had chosen a route which crossed a small rather shallow gully below which old avalanche debris was still visible. The combined weight of both men on the slope was sufficient to release the slab which carried them down. By swimming, the second man managed to stay close to the surface. Finding no sign of his companion he limped back down to the road on one ski to raise the alarm. The rescue group, hardly recovered from their morning's exertions were at the scene within three-quarters of an hour, but despite a dog search and careful probing, the body wasn't found until late that evening, lying face down with an ice crust around the head.

For the weary dejected searchers it was a long ski down in the dark to the road; the welcoming news that two climbers were missing on Mount Thompson was hardly guaranteed to raise their spirits. It was too late to do anything that night but at first light they were all gathered on the Wapta Icefields helping in the recovery of two more bodies. That wasn't the end of it: the same afternoon a report came in that three heli-skiers had been buried by a large avalanche in the Purcell Mountains and would they stand-by.

The Anatomy of an Avalanche Accident

Three "experienced" skiers left the majority of their group skiing on the flats around the Lodge and headed out for a tour to a popular high mountain lake. Conditions were picture perfect, with cloudless skies and mild temperatures. *"We won't need our transceivers, we're only going to the lake"*.

Alf and his three friends *"...wanted a carefree, easy going kind of trip and a fairly short day of skiing"*. After discussing potential avalanche hazard on the drive to the mountain they decided to head for the same high mountain lake. *"Even so, we carried avalanche transceivers, snow shovels, avalanche probe poles, a first aid kit and spare clothing with us as a matter of course."*

The local stability forecast indicated *"Stability decreasing. Soft slab with buried surface hoar — difficult to detect"*. It went on to add *"Safe routefinding imperative due to a weakening snowpack and warm tempera-*
tures. Slopes which have not recently avalanched should be considered as suspect."

The ski into the lake was fast and easy; wax was working and the trail was in good shape. There were tracks from other groups leading to a sunny, gladed plateau above the lake; a fine spot for lunch.

Beyond the plateau an attractive-looking snow-filled basin leads up to a col between the main peak and its much lower outlier. The "experienced" group *"...found some fresh ski tracks leading up the ridge between the lake and this basin"* and followed them. After a short distance one of the party decided to turn back and wait for the other two at the lake.

They followed the tracks up through tightly packed trees and *"decided to carry on to find a clear run out rather than ski down through the trees. We followed the existing ski tracks around the south-west ridge and came out at treeline halfway up from the valley below."*

Meanwhile, Alf's party lunched at the open gladed plateau above the lake and *"...discussed the option of following the tracks into the basin and decided it might be worth a look."* Because it appeared that the

Fig. 2 An overall view of the area described in the "The Anatomy of an Avalanche Accident". The avalanche ran down the gully below the col in the centre of the picture. Alf's group were at the top of the treed ridge on the left of the gully. The slide started on the slope above the top of the trees to the right of the gully.

other group would either be forced to lose the elevation they were gaining, or they would have to continue in a mid-slope traverse across steep terrain, Alf decided to choose an easier route through the forest to the bottom of the basin.

The lower section of the basin is divided by a treed ridge, splitting the basin into two gullies. The entire ridge line along the western and northern perimeter of the basin was crowned by very well developed cornices, indicating heavy wind loading of the slopes in the basin, while the south-west facing slopes on the east side of the basin showed evidence of cross-loading.

On emerging from the trees at the bottom of the most easterly gully Alf's group decided that this gully was a potential terrain trap. *"We double-checked that all of our transceivers were transmitting and then probed the snow with our ski poles. We could feel approximately 25 cm of firm snow with a weak layer underneath."*

Proceeding a few metres farther to get a better view, one of the Alf's party, a qualified heli-ski guide, *"...did not like the 'hollow, drum-like' sound of the snow as we crossed onto the south-west-facing aspect. Given this information we decided not to ski this half of the basin at all."*

Fig. 3 The photograph mentioned in the text, taken a few minutes before the avalanche released. Photo by Alf Skrastins.

Fig. 4 A view of the avalanche site. The slope angle where the skiers triggered the slide is 35°. The average slope angle in the top portion of the gully is 36°. Photo by George Field.

"We briefly discussed avalanche hazards, noting that a large cornice was an apparent threat to both the valley floor and to the south-east aspect of the valley. We noted that the south-west aspect of the valley did not offer any apparent threat (there was no indication of avalanche activity and there were clusters of trees extending well above us."

One of them probed with his ski pole and felt that the snow was fairly consolidated. *"We decided to continue to a group of trees 40 m above; we had no intention of carrying on to open slopes beyond."* At the top of the trees, the slope ascended by Alf's party was wind-scoured and they were in a safe position. While stopped to take a photo Alf noticed 2 skiers following the tracks made by an earlier party. *"They had just made the switchback at the bottom of the convex roll in the upper portion of the gully. As they approached the switchback at the top of the roll I took a photograph of them and then put my camera away. I was about 200 m distant and 20 to 30 m higher than the skiers."*

Instead they followed the treed ground in the middle of the basin in order to get high enough for a good view of the area and to check out the other half of the basin. The heli-ski guide did a quick shovel shear test in the top 70 cm of the snowpack on the south-east aspect. The column of snow sheared very easily at about 40 cm below the surface while she was still in the process of isolating the column. *"At that point we decided to avoid the open slopes altogether and to stick to the treed areas."*

About 30 metres above them, and across the gully on the south-west aspect, the two skiers had stopped to decide whether to go farther up or to turn around. From here the existing tracks divided; one set going up the valley floor to the col, the other set traversing the south-west facing slope towards the mountain.

One of the skiers fell while making the switchback at the top of the roll. When he got up they appeared to be having a discussion. As they continued towards a clump of trees a short distance away, a crack appeared in the snow between the skiers and the trees.

The initial size of the avalanche was small, a slab about 15 metres square, and released with no warning. *"I believe we were standing right on, or next to, the trigger point. We were immediately thrown on our sides and had no chance to ski off the slope."*

"The skier on the right landed with his head slightly uphill and immediately pulled his skis underneath himself and used his arms to keep his upper body off the snow. The other skier fell with his head downhill and appeared to just hold his position on the snow and to look up at the slope behind him."

9

"The slab broke up and the slab I was on missed the trees and carried me 50 m down the slope and began to slow down. At that point I thought the avalanche was over. However this small slide triggered the rest of the slope."

Alf watched in horror. "The crack ran up the slope from the trees for about 60 m, then cut across the slope towards the ridge line and then ran just below the ridge crest and below the cornice at the col. It widened very quickly as it ran. It was as if cloth were being ripped or a zipper were being opened. This was accompanied by a hissing sound, like air being let out of a big bag and a blanket being dragged across sand ... all at the same time."

"I looked over my shoulder to see the entire wall of the valley above begin to move. The slab I was on picked up speed again and disintegrated. I was lying on my back and using my arms to try to 'swim' upright."

"The skiers were moving slowly downslope and the snow they were on was starting to break up as they moved. However the snow on the steeper slope above them was moving faster than the snow they were on, and began to ride up over the top of the slab they were on."

"The upright skier frantically pulled himself up on top of the slabs as they descended onto him. The other skier seemed unable to prevent the first of these faster slabs from covering him."

"Successive waves of snow from the higher slopes over-ran the snow in the middle of the main slide which ran down the main south-west-facing slope and into the gully. At the same time, a much thicker layer of snow from the slope directly below the col was also sliding in an easterly direction, running over the rest of the debris. This phase of the slide was accompanied by the low rumbling sound usually associated with avalanches." After another 100 m the avalanche stopped.

"My head remained above the snow during the entire slide. When the snow stopped my legs were buried to above my knees. I had lost one pole, my hat and glasses. My skis were still attached but were twisted around at an awkward angle. I was unhurt."

When the slide stopped Alf's group could no longer see the skiers. "I skied down the tree protected ridge, looking down into the gully when possible. After a few turns I could see one skier on top of the snow at the very bottom of the slide."

When he reached the bottom ("I descended within the trees a bit farther to avoid crossing a short, steep slope") the skier on the surface was sitting on the debris, facing downhill, digging out his lower legs. There was no sign of the other skier. The guide was running back and forth down the debris looking for some sign of the missing skier.

After completing the initial search, and with only two hours of daylight left, Alf, whose skis were closest to the bottom, went for help while the others probed likely locations.

"We suspected that since I had ridden the avalanche unhurt and on the surface all the way to the toe of the slide, something drastically different must have happened to my companion. Our initial probing was therefore directed at the trees below his entry point, and at a large deep pile of debris lower down where the larger avalanche had intersected the initial avalanche."

He was found two hours later by a rescue team face down under 70-100 cm of snow, his pack on but missing both skis. He did not appear to have struggled at all.

"I should note that my friend and I had over 30 years of combined backcountry skiing experience, but despite this we failed to recognize the danger of the slope we were on."

"Because of our approach line through the trees on the south-west ridge, which obscured our overall view of the slope and potential avalanche patterns, the danger of the slope was far less obvious to us than to parties which approach the valley from the valley floor. Combined with the results of our pole probe, the fresh ski tracks already on the slope, and our decision to remain in the trees, these circumstances misled us to believe the slope had low risk of avalanche."

Introduction

Snow avalanches are the greatest source of danger for mountain travellers in winter. They catch and very often kill the unwary who literally trigger their own destiny when they venture onto unsafe snow slopes in a moment of inattention or ignorance.

Historically, avalanche victims came from among those people who lived and worked in the shadow of the great mountains; whose houses, even whole villages were destroyed every generation or two by catastrophic slides considered to be "Acts of God" and so to be suffered with fortitude. Today, the most common victim is the climber, the ski tourer, and the backcountry powder-hound.

Since 1950 at least 400 climbers and skiers have died in avalanches in the U.S.A. and Canada. In a 1975 report on avalanche fatalities in the United States, Knox Williams attributes the recent increase in deaths to the fact that *"More and more people — many with little or no avalanche awareness training — are venturing into steep mountain terrain."*

The public generally associates avalanche accidents with skiers. This is far from true: climbers, often experienced mountaineers of the first rank, figure high in avalanche accident statistics. Research indicates that few climbers are able to recognize avalanche terrain let alone identify snow conditions conducive to avalanching. And because climbers are often roped together many accidents involve the whole party. The risk of taking a fall when climbing is known and generally accepted; each person climbs at his own safe level using whatever method of protection he thinks necessary. In the vast majority of avalanche accidents, however, the recognition, evaluation and qualified acceptance of risk is absent; victims are often totally unaware of the danger. **Only by recognizing risk** can you use your knowledge and experience to reduce that risk to an acceptable level. Back in 1923, F.A. Collins wrote in his book Mountain Climbing, *"The experienced mountaineer learns to judge snow conditions with marvelous accuracy and becomes so confident of his opinion that he will risk his life on his judgement."*

Avalanches are complex natural phenomena and in spite of modern technology and years of research no one can predict with certainty when or if an avalanche will run. Avalanches may occur on any steep snow covered slope. How steep, and how much snow is required to initiate a slide are but two of the many factors to be considered when evaluating hazard. Another complication is that snow conditions vary in different geographical locations and at different times of the year. There is a vast difference between the fluffy powder snow of Colorado and the heavy, wet snow of Washington's Olympic Range.

Some winter seasons produce an inordinate number of avalanche accidents. Frank Smythe, the British mountaineer and author, writing in the 1929 Alpine Journal theorized that years of low early snowfall and high winds in the Alps were accountable for the worst recreational avalanche casualties on record. Conversely, he noted that in seasons of heavy early snowfall and little wind there were few accidents. There is solid fact behind his theorizing: wind and a shallow snowpack has a great deal to do with avalanche accidents as you will learn. For instance, the 1976-77 season in the Canadian Rockies — a cold winter of unusually low snowfall — produced a rash of avalanche incidents and between February 4th and March 5th, 1992 fourteen people died in avalanches in the western United States — a result of heavy snowfall in February on a shallower than usual snowpack weakened by depth hoar.

What are your chances of being caught in an avalanche and what might be the consequences? If you are a cross-country skier travelling on light touring skis along a marked trail chances are that you'll never have a problem. Because of equipment limitations you'll rarely venture onto the steeper slopes and so unconsciously avoid avalanche hazard by sticking to flatter terrain. It is the ski tourers, touring off valley trails over high alpine passes, telemark skiers, and ski mountaineers and climbers who are most at risk.

The majority of victims trigger the slide themselves. The chance of being caught by a naturally triggered slide is remote unless you are travelling during or immediately after a heavy snowfall or are climbing in the higher ranges of the world. Gerald Seligman in his book "Snow Structures and Ski Fields" published in 1936 quotes an old Swiss guide as saying, *"I never fear that any avalanche will catch me unless I have myself brought it down"*.

Fig. 5 Snowboarders are recent additions to those at risk of avalanches in the backcountry. Boarders are capable of tackling any slope a skier would ski. Boards, because of their large surface area stress the snowpack less than skis.

Statistically, the more time you spend high in the mountains the more chance you have of being involved in an avalanche accident either to your own party or to another group.

The answer to the second question, *"What might be the consequences ?"*, can be found in a few statistics extracted from accident reports compiled both in Europe and in North America. Although these reports differ in detail there are a number of significant similarities. Seventy to eighty percent of people caught in avalanches are skiers and climbers. Approximately 50% to 60% survived, and of those who did survive, 60% either freed themselves or were found because some part of their body or equipment was protruding above the surface of the snow. Of the people completely buried, only a dismal 20% to 25% lived to tell of the ordeal.

All the statisticians seem to agree that if a person is buried under more than 2 metres of snow the chances of survival are almost nil. The weight of snow above the victim and the time it takes to dig down to him make survival unlikely in the majority of cases.

The most disturbing statistic, and the most important one for you to bear in mind, is the time factor. Again figures vary, but not by much. If you are buried you have an 80% chance of survival if located within a few minutes of the avalanche coming to rest. European statistics show that for every hour an avalanche victim spends under the snow the chance of survival is cut by half. For example, your chance is 40% after 1 hour, 20% after 2 hours and so on. North American figures, which contain a far higher proportion of back-country victims, are much more frightening. They show that after half an hour the chance of survival is down to about 50%. There are documented cases of victims being dead after burials of as little as 15 minutes! Obviously, your first priority is to avoid being caught by an avalanche in the first place, but should the unthinkable happen, your greatest chance of survival lies in your companions locating you and digging you out in the fastest possible time.

If you study published case histories of avalanche accidents you'll become aware of a number of similarities between back-country accidents. **A large percentage of accidents occurred when avalanche hazard was known to be high.** In some cases the victims chose to ignore warnings and proceed with their trip; in others the victims were completely unaware of the possibility of avalanches. Many victims didn't know how to pick a safe route through avalanche terrain or, conversely were unable to recognize potentially dangerous slopes. Few of those involved had any experience in evaluating avalanche hazard, even victims considered experienced leaders. Knox Williams, in his portrait of a typical avalanche victim says, *"The victim is a male, 27 years old, has had several years of skiing or mountaineering experience, and didn't know an avalanche from a snowball."*

This book stresses the avoidance of avalanche hazard by good routefinding, by recognition and the consequent avoidance of hazardous slopes and by staying out of avalanche terrain during periods when avalanche hazard is high.

However, it recognizes that days when the snow is stable far outnumber days when it is unstable and that there are telemark skiers, extreme skiers and snowboarders who want some guidance on skiing safely in avalanche terrain. It therefore tries to address the difficult problem of evaluating snow stability for the backcountry powder seeker and makes some recommendations on techniques to use when skiing steep backcountry slopes. But it can only point the way; you must go out into the mountains and practice what you learn here. André Roch, in a 1979 address to some of the world's leaders in avalanche research put it very succinctly when he said, *"Remember this, my friends, the avalanche does not know that you are an expert!"*

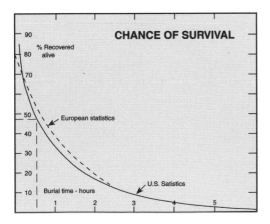

Fig. 2. After half an hour under the snow your chance of survival is reduced to about 50%

Fig. 1.1 In times of instability, good travel practices and careful routefinding is required to travel safely in avalanche terrain. Cariboo Mountains, British Columbia. Photo by Alf Skrastins.

1

Travel in Avalanche Terrain

Whenever you are skiing or climbing in an area with snow slopes steep enough to slide you are travelling in avalanche terrain and must consider the possibility and consequences of an avalanche. Most people forget that avalanches are not limited to the winter season; a small, 5 cm deep sluff of wet summer snow which carries a climber over the edge of a cliff can be just as fatal as a skier-triggered 50 cm deep slab avalanche in the winter.

The basic law of safe travel is **Avoid hazardous areas**. For avalanches to occur snow must lie on slopes steep enough to allow it to slide, so it follows that if steep slopes are avoided by careful routefinding most hazardous situations can be avoided. If you consider that most cross-country skiers follow trails along valley bottoms then this concept of avoiding steep slopes is, in practice, quite realistic. Except during periods of extreme instability, which are usually predictable, avalanches rarely fall on the traveller of their own accord.

If you're going to be climbing higher up into the mountains where the terrain is both steeper and potentially more dangerous, you'll need to study the finer points of stability evaluation. You must:

— **Determine the current and possible future avalanche hazard in the area**.

— Pick a safe route based on the above knowledge.

— **Be prepared** to cope with emergencies due to fatigue, benightment, equipment failures, weather, and avalanches.

Safe Travel

A number of basic precepts for safe travel in mountainous terrain (and therefore by definition, avalanche terrain) have developed over a century or more of mountaineering. While you may choose to break or ignore some of these rules as a calculated risk in order to achieve a particular goal, you should do so with a full knowledge of what you are doing and the extent of the risks you are taking.

Avalanche Warning Programs

Many alpine areas, both in Europe and North America, have organized avalanche warning programs as a public service. While they differ in detail the programs all provide warnings at times of extreme hazard and disseminate information through the news media, via recorded telephone messages, and through bulletins available at Park offices and downhill ski areas.

In France, Germany and some areas of Austria bulletins are issued daily. Other Alpine countries issue bulletins on Fridays, with intermediate reports if the situation changes. In the United States and Canada advisories are usually issued daily and, if rapidly changing conditions warrant it, are updated several times a day. In North America warnings don't usually apply to downhill ski areas where control work is carried out.

An attempt has been made to standardize the terminology used in avalanche hazard reports. Many avalanche professionals feel that the use of the term "Hazard" is confusing and syntactically incorrect and that ratings using snow instability in terms of natural and human-triggered avalanches are more appropriate.

Unfortunately, the brief, standard descriptions, if used alone, are insufficient for the backcountry skier. Consider the definition of "Moderate Instability".

"**Moderate Instability** Areas of unstable snow. Natural and human-triggered avalanches are possible on steep, snow-covered slopes and gullies."

This definition is used in more forecasts than any other, and represents snow conditions when some of the best powder skiing is available. It gives no indication of which slopes are likely to be stable nor does it give any guidance on whether the skier should stay below treeline or venture onto steeper, higher elevation slopes.

Some of the more enlightened Avalanche Information Centres are now issuing bulletins which tell their clients what is happening in the backcountry in an entertaining and thought-provoking manner. They are written in an anecdotal style, using terms the backcountry skier can understand (see the sample bulletins opposite).

In practice the user needs to know:

— The overall instability rating for the area.

— The probability of triggering a slide.

— What aspects of slope are affected.

— What degree of slope may be suspect.

— Above or below treeline.

— Is instability localized or widespread.

— Have slides already occurred in the area.

Remember that most snow stability reports cover a fairly large area and that individual slopes in that area may still be dangerous, even when the overall hazard is low.

Obtaining Avalanche Hazard Reports

Avalanche hazard reports should be a major consideration in deciding whether or not to go ahead with a trip. It may be better to wait for more favorable conditions.

Any winter travel in the backcountry should begin with a call to the local Forest, Park or Recreation Area office to obtain the latest weather forecast and snow report. Find out the phone number for recorded telephone messages in your area and get into the habit of calling frequently so as to keep track of snow conditions throughout the season. Other possible sources are ski patrols, ski areas and local radio and newspaper reports.

GOOD MORNING, THIS IS TOM KIMBROUGH WITH BACKCOUNTRY AVALANCHE AND MOUNTAIN WEATHER INFORMATION AT 7:30 AM ON TUESDAY, JANUARY 9, 1990.

THE UTAH AVALANCHE FORECAST CENTER IS A COOPERATIVE EFFORT BETWEEN THE FOREST SERVICE AND THE NATIONAL WEATHER SERVICE.

ALL AREAS:
MY PARTNER BRAD AND I HAD AN EXCITING TIME PROWLING AROUND IN THE OGDEN MOUNTAINS YESTERDAY. IT WAS JUST LIKE YOU HEAR ABOUT IN THE AVALANCHE CLASSES, WITH CRACKING IN THE NEW SNOW, LOUD WHOOMPING SOUNDS, AND BIG COLLAPSES. WE WERE DIGGING SNOWPITS ON VARIOUS SLOPES AND TIMIDLY NOSING ON TO STEEPER TERRAIN. BRAD WAS OUT ON A 30 DEGREE SLOPE DIGGING ANOTHER HOLE, WITH ME WATCHING HIM, WHEN THE WHOLE SLOPE COLLAPSED AND A LARGE SLIDE RELEASED ON THE 35 DEGREE GULLY ABOUT 50 FEET IN FRONT OF BRAD.

WE WERE FINDING A FIRM SLAB OF NEW SNOW ABOUT A FOOT AND A HALF TO TWO FEET DEEP THAT WAS RELEASING ON THE WEAK SUGAR SNOW THAT WAS ON THE GROUND DURING THE HOLIDAYS.

YESTERDAY, ABOUT A FOOT OF HEAVY, WET SNOW FELL AND THERE WERE STRONG WINDS ALONG THE RIDGES. THIS HAS INCREASED THE AVALANCHE HAZARD TO HIGH ON MANY SLOPES. AN AVALANCHE WARNING IS IN EFFECT FOR THE WASATCH MOUNTAINS TODAY.

WE CONSIDER THE HAZARD OF HUMAN TRIGGERED AVALANCHES TO BE HIGH ON MANY SLOPES STEEPER THAN 35 DEGREES. NORTHWEST, NORTH, AND EAST FACING SLOPES ABOVE 7000 FEET, WHERE THE UNDERLYING SNOWPACK IS WEAK WILL BE THE MOST DANGEROUS, BUT UNSTABLE AREAS WILL EXIST ON OTHER SLOPES, ESPECIALLY ONES WITH DEPOSITS OF WIND DRIFTED SNOW. BACKCOUNTRY TRAVELLERS WITHOUT GOOD ROUTE FINDING AND SNOW STABILITY SKILLS SHOULD AVOID SLOPES STEEPER THAN 30 DEGREES.

WARM TEMPERATURES MAY ALSO CAUSE WET SLIDE ACTIVITY ON SLOPES BELOW 7,000.

MOUNTAIN WEATHER:
SKIES WILL BE CLEARING TODAY AS A RIDGE OF HIGH PRESSURE BUILDS OVER THE WEST COAST. TEMPERATURES WILL REMAIN WARM, WITH A HIGH AT 7,000 FEET NEAR 40 DEGREES TODAY. WINDS WILL BE LIGHT FROM THE WEST. WEDNESDAY WILL AGAIN BE PARTLY CLOUDY. BY THE WEEKEND, THERE IS AGAIN A CHANCE OF SNOW.

I WANT TO REMIND YOU THAT SEVERAL GOOD AVALANCHE CLASSES ARE BEING OFFERED THIS SEASON INCLUDING THE EXCELLENT ALASKA AVALANCHE SCHOOL THIS COMING WEEKEND. CALL US FOR DETAILS ON ANY OF THESE CLASSES.

IF YOU WOULD LIKE MORE DETAILED INFORMATION CALL XXX-XXXX. IF YOU SEE ANYTHING OF INTEREST, CALL US IN THE OFFICE AT XXX-XXXX OR 1-800-XXX-XXXX.

GOOD MORNING, THIS IS BRAD MEIKLEJOHN WITH YOUR BACKCOUNTRY AVALANCHE AND MOUNTAIN WEATHER INFORMATION AT 4:30 PM ON FRIDAY, FEBRUARY 9, 1990.

THE UTAH AVALANCHE FORECAST CENTER IS A COOPERATIVE EFFORT BETWEEN THE WASATCH-CACHE NATIONAL FOREST AND THE NATIONAL WEATHER SERVICE.

A FEW HOURS AFTER I PUT OUT THE FORECAST THIS MORNING I FOUND OUT THAT THERE HAD BEEN A BACKCOUNTRY SKIER CAUGHT IN AN AVALANCHE ON THURSDAY IN DAY'S FORK. THE SLIDE WAS IN A STEEP NORTH FACING CHUTE NEAR 10,000' AND BROKE OUT 2.5' DEEP AND 20' WIDE. THE SKIER WAS CAUGHT AND CARRIED ON A ROUGH RIDE, BUT ENDED UP ON TOP WITH ONE BROKEN SKI AND ONE LOST SKI.

IN ADDITION TO THIS SLIDE, THERE WERE SOME LARGE SLIDES THAT BROKE OUT UP TO 6' DEEP WITH AVALANCHE CONTROL WORK IN LITTLE COTTONWOOD CANYON YESTERDAY AND TODAY. THESE LAST PLACES WERE ONES THAT HAD BEEN HEAVILY LOADED WITH WIND BLOWN SNOW.

IT HAS BEEN SNOWING LIGHTLY TODAY, BUT ONLY A TRACE TO AN INCH PILED UP, AND THE WINDS HAVE BEEN 10-20 MPH FROM THE WEST ALL DAY. IT LOOKS LIKE WE WILL HAVE CLOUDS AGAIN TONIGHT, WITH SOME LIGHT SNOW ON SATURDAY MORNING. SUNDAY AND MONDAY SHOULD BE NICE DAYS, FOLLOWED BY MORE SNOW ON TUESDAY.

A COUPLE OF THINGS HAVE BEEN BOTHERING ME LATELY- THE FIRST IS THAT I KEEP MEETING PEOPLE IN THE BACKCOUNTRY WHO SAY THINGS LIKE "THE AVALANCHE CENTER SAID IT IS MODERATE, DUDE, LET'S PUNCH IT" DO YOU REALLY KNOW WHAT WE MEAN BY MODERATE? MODERATE AVALANCHE HAZARD IS NOT A GREEN LIGHT, IT'S A YELLOW LIGHT. IT MEANS THAT ONE OUT OF EVERY TEN SLOPES IS DANGEROUS AND COULD KILL YOU.

THE SECOND THING IS THAT PEOPLE ARE EMBARRASSED TO CALL US AFTER THEY HAVE BEEN IN A SLIDE. PLEASE DON'T BE EMBARRASSED. WE WON'T BROADCAST YOUR NAME, AND THE INFORMATION YOU GIVE US MAY SAVE SOME ELSE'S LIFE.

THERE IS STILL A MODERATE OR LOCALIZED HAZARD OF HUMAN-TRIGGERED AVALANCHES ON UPPER-ELEVATION WIND LOADED SLOPES, AS WELL AS A MODERATE HAZARD OF DEEPER SLIDES ON NORTH AND EAST FACING SLOPES ABOVE 9000' AND STEEPER THAN 35 DEGREES. THE HAZARD OF A HUMAN TRIGGERED SLIDE IS GENERALLY LOW IN ALL OTHER AREAS.

A MODERATE HAZARD DAY MEANS YOU SHOULD LOOK CAREFULLY AT EACH SLOPE YOU PLAN TO SKI, DIG SOME SNOWPITS, DO SOME STABILITY TESTS, AND DON'T GET CARRIED AWAY BY POWDER FEVER.

THE BEST SNOW IS ON MID-ELEVATION PROTECTED SLOPES, WHILE THE UPPER ELEVATION SNOW GOT WIND BLASTED AND THE SOUTH FACES NOW HAVE A CRUST,

Fig. 1.2 Two sample Backcountry Avalanche and Mountain Weather Bulletin from the Utah Avalanche Forecast Center. Note the anecdotal style used by the forecasters to add credibility to their report which is aimed at the young well-educated recreationists in their area. Courtesy Brad Meiklejohn and the Utah Avalanche Forecast Center.

Planning

Being prepared is one of the basic principles of winter mountain travel. If you have not done the tour or climb before find out as much as you can about it beforehand. Use guide books, accounts in journals and magazines, and the advice of friends as sources of information. Plan your route on a map, determine how far it is and how much time it is likely to take. Do you have enough daylight to allow a suitable safety margin?

In some areas such as Forest Reserves and National Parks you may be required to register your trip with the authorities. If no formal means of registration exists then leave word with some responsible person about the route you will be taking and your expected time of return.

If, during the tour, you are faced with a tricky routefinding decision, take your time. Get out a map and look around. Don't be rushed into making a hasty decision. If you are leading a party don't be too proud to ask for another opinion and discuss alternative routes with your companions. A large proportion of mountain accidents, including avalanche accidents, happen as the direct or indirect result of two errors of judgement: late starts and poor routefinding

Leadership of Club Groups

Outdoor clubs owe it to their membership to provide competent leadership for their outdoor activities. Records of avalanche accidents show that many of the so called competent leaders used by clubs, experienced mountaineers even, had little or no knowledge of safe travel in avalanche terrain.

Good leadership is absolutely necessary if large parties of mixed ability are to travel safely. The following outline issued a few years ago by Banff National Park wardens for ski tourers describes the duties of a party leader. It's inserted as a reminder to club leaders and also as a checklist for people who are deciding whether or not to go out on a trip with a certain leader.

Plan the trip thoroughly. Not only the route, but the equipment to be carried by the party.

Evaluate each member's capacity and ability, adjusting the severity of the trip to the ability of the party's weakest member.

Check the personal equipment of the party to ensure that everyone is adequately equipped.

Pace the travel speed of the party so that no one becomes exhausted. Amateur leaders often try to burn off the rest of the group.

Keep the party together: but not too close in avalanche terrain. Large groups require a "Tail-end-Charlie". Frequent stops and counts of the party must be made, especially when skiing downhill.

Route selection. The leader should be experienced in route selection.

Snowcraft. The leader should have a thorough knowledge of mountain weather, snowcraft and avalanche hazard evaluation.

Navigation. The leader must be capable of travelling with map and compass in whiteout conditions.

Repairs. Ensure that there are sufficient tools in the group to repair broken skis, skins and bindings. After late starts, broken equipment is the next most common indirect cause of accidents.

Rescue. The leader must be capable of organizing a back-country avalanche rescue, of applying first aid, and of keeping survivors alive until rescuers arrive.

Travelling Alone

Don't travel alone off frequented trails in avalanche terrain. *"A ski tourer travelling alone in the backcountry near Taos Ski Valley, New Mexico, triggered and was buried by a soft slab avalanche. Rescuers instantly spotted a ski tip sticking from the snow and made a quick recovery of his body from under 2 feet of snow. The victim had died of suffocation, a death that would have easily been prevented had he not been travelling alone."*

The Party

The correct speed of travel for any party is the speed of the slowest member. Bearing this in mind, select a party able to travel at approximately the same rate. Conditioning and ability may make up for lack of experience or conversely, sheer doggedness make up for lack of skiing ability. On the whole though, an inexperienced person, out of condition and with little skiing ability will slow a party down considerably. I am not suggesting that this person should be left behind but rather that the party should lower its objectives and allow more time for the trip.

It's very important in avalanche terrain that the party travel as a cohesive unit. No one should go so far ahead of the main party that he's only seen at lunch stops. Nor should a person be allowed to fall behind to the extent that he looses sight of the person in front for more than a few minutes. This rule becomes more important as the weather deteriorates; those in front tend to press on faster and faster while the slower members of the group at the back slow down even more. In such cases the leader must use considerable constraint in controlling his tendency to rush ahead. Both psychologically and from the point of view of keeping warm, it's better to slow down the pace than have to stop and wait. Encourage the buddy system when skiing down through trees, where skiers pair up and keep in touch with each other all the way down.

Pick a Safe Trail

If there is a warning of high or extreme avalanche hazard in effect then you should either discard more ambitious plans and pick a completely safe trail or stay at home. Completely safe trails are those which do not cross over or underneath any slope which is steep enough to generate an avalanche. Even if you consider yourself competent in hazard evaluation take note of extreme avalanche hazard warnings; are your predictions likely to be more accurate than those of the professional hazard forecaster?

Avoid Steep Slopes

When a moderate hazard warning is in effect, it's generally acceptable to risk skiing trails which cross the runout zones of avalanche paths. Although the chance of being caught by an avalanche is very slight, you should still take the basic precaution of travelling 50 to 100 metres apart on wide slopes and cross narrow slopes one at a time. Avoid slopes of over 25 degrees; in other words any slope the average cross-country skier would think twice about skiing down on skinny skis. The safest routes are valley bottoms and the tops of ridges.

Food and Drink

Eat and drink regularly during the day. Too many people feel they can exist on a candy bar and a hand-full of nuts and make up the deficiency when the trip's over. In an avalanche emergency it's important that survivors have the sufficient reserve of energy needed to help search for the victims.

Fig. 1.3 When avalanche hazard is extreme, temper your ambitions by selecting a trail which avoids all avalanche terrain. Photo by Gillean Daffern

Rest Stops

Stop well away from the runout zones of potential avalanche slopes. This may sound obvious, but families out ski touring have a habit of stopping for lunch on large open slopes with a good view, happily oblivious of the avalanche slopes above them.

Camp Sites

Avoid setting up camp below a slope which could accumulate enough snow to slide. Because slab avalanches can originate on slopes as shallow as 25°, the danger is not always obvious: during the search for 2 students on Mount St. Helens in 1975, *"the majority of the experienced rescue personnel appeared little concerned of the possibility of another avalanche even with the knowledge that at least one had occurred just two and a half days before."* Such a slope rising above the camp established by a beginners Snow and Ice School on the Forsythe Glacier was becoming unstable: warm weather in the middle of the month had created a surface crust. Then, between the 23rd and 25th of April, about 50 cm of snow fell accompanied by a slight drop in temperature. Early on the 26th, the day the 29 climbers were toiling upwards to the campsite, the sky cleared and the temperature rose. It would have been a fine day but for the wind which was gathering strength; in fact by the time the tents were up and snow caves built, a strong gusty cross-wind was piling loose snow up against the tents and conditions were so unpleasant that plans for a crevasse rescue practice were postponed. By now the slope above was in prime condition to avalanche and at twenty six minutes past eight, some 500 metres above the camp, a soft slab released and came pouring down onto the camp trapping most people inside their tents, either burying them or pushing them down the slope as it swept by. Fast action by the survivors probing with anything at hand such as ice axes and tent poles saved many lives.

When speculating why some people lived and others died some interesting observations were made about the siting of tents. Those placed on cut-and-fill platforms (the angle of the slope was 28°) were propelled down the slope and only partially buried. Other tents dug 2 metres into the slope were completely buried; all but one of their occupants died. Snow caves were unaffected, although one entrance was blocked and had to be cleared from the outside. This serves as a reminder to take shovels inside a snow cave with you.

Although snow caves are potentially safe on steep slopes where there is a chance of slides coming down from above, you must be extremely careful in your choice of slope. Don't dig into slab and don't site them in gullies which are natural chutes for avalanches and stonefall. In certain conditions even the top of a snow gully is hazardous: consider what happened to 4 climbers during a winter attempt on the East Ridge of Mount Edith Cavell (Canadian Rockies). All afternoon, they had been climbing up a long snow gully parallel to the usual summer route. Around 5 pm, now close to the top, they decided to bivouac. The deep layers of drifted snow in the gully were supported by a weak layer of depth hoar next to the ground which, though capable of sustaining the weight of the climbers, collapsed during the deeper excavation of the snow cave. Unnoticed by the climbers, the instability of the snowpack had been further decreased by a substantial rise of temperature throughout the day. The resulting avalanche swept the climbers back down the gully and killed three of them.

Ridges are usually safe, but be wary of camping below the lee slope of a ridge. An accident in the New Zealand Alps in the winter of 1966 had several unusual features which are worth thinking about. A rescue party was out searching for a group of 4 climbers missing on Mount Rolleston in Arthur's Pass National Park. The weather was atrocious; heavy snow, the first of the winter, was being piled on lee slopes by the prevailing north-westerly winds. The rescuers pitched camp on a small spur abutting against a face below the summit ridge of the mountain. The face, which lay on the windward side of the ridge, was a perfectly safe route to the summit; the party climbed up and down it all the next day. On the second evening the

Fig. 1.4 This relatively shallow slope was the site of the Mount St. Helens accident (see opposite page) in which 5 people died when their camp was overwhelmed by a slab avalanche. Note signs of further avalanching on adjacent slopes. Photo by Ronald V. Emetaz, courtesy U.S. Forest Service.

storm ended. With the cessation of snow came an unexpected change in wind direction; it began to blow hard out of the south, moving snow previously dumped on the southern glacier over the summit ridge onto the previously safe face. A cornice developed and a large area of slab below that. Sometime in the middle of the night, only a few hours after it's formation, the slab released. Although most of the avalanche parted on hitting the spur, sliding harmlessly down either side of it, one wave of snow washed over the top burying tents to a depth of 2 to 3 metres. One man sleeping in the tent closest to the face died.

Turning Back

There are two basic safety reasons for turning back from your tour. First, if you are obviously not going to be able to make it out by dark. An impromptu benightment, while inconvenient in summer, is much more serious in winter. Second, if there is evidence of serious instability in the snowpack such as signs of recent avalanching on the slopes around you. Only if you are certain of not venturing into avalanche terrain should you go on.

Often a decision to turn back can involve a lot of mental courage, especially on the part of the leader of an organized group. No one really likes to turn back unless they are cold and miserable, and on a warm sunny day few people even think of avalanche hazard. If you do decide to retreat, explain your reasons to the whole party.

Fig. 1.5 The extent of the fatal slab avalanche near Citadel Pass is clearly seen on the photograph. The usual route crosses the ridge above the steep slopes. Photo by Bruno Engler.

Travel During Storm

Sometimes there's no alternative but to travel through avalanche terrain during a heavy snow storm. Since the greatest danger from avalanches is during or immediately after the storm, make an extra effort to reach safety during the first few hours of snowfall. Observe the build-up of snow and note the direction of the wind. Avoid the vicinity of steeper slopes which may be subject to direct action avalanches. Pay particular attention to routefinding — difficult enough in a whiteout — so you don't wander onto suspect slopes unintentionally. Travel will be slowed down and there will be a tendency for the party to bunch up, exposing the whole party to danger at one time.

Consider what happened to a guided party of 24 skiers in the Citadel Pass area of Banff National Park a few years ago. The party, skiing to a helicopter rendezvous during a blizzard, was off the normal route which crosses an exposed open ridge and was embarked on a more sheltered route below timberline. Although the party had triggered a small slide earlier on in the traverse which carried one member of the party down the slope for 30 metres, the guide elected to carry on along the same high line; he had arranged to meet the helicopter in the late afternoon. The weather was now worsening; it was snowing heavily and visibility was reduced to a few metres, effectively hiding the steep slopes above. At 2:00 pm, as the party were skiing across a sparsely-timbered hillside, the slope fractured high above them and a large avalanche flowed down through the trees taking with it 7 skiers and completely burying 5 of them. Hurried probing uncovered 4 of the victims almost immediately, but the fifth person, a woman, was not recovered until an estimated 30 to 45 minutes after the accident. By this time she had died of suffocation.

This incident is a prime example of bad route selection during extremely hazardous avalanche conditions. After the first avalanche, which indicated beyond all doubt the instability of the snowpack, the guide should have re-assessed his proposed route, taking instead a longer but lower line across gentler slopes even if this meant being late for the rendezvous. Once the original mistake had been made, two other factors contributed to the tragedy: the party had closed up because of bad weather and the party were not carrying rescue beacons because the normal route which they were to have taken didn't warrant their use. If they had been used, it's probable the victim would have been recovered much faster and might still be alive today.

Summer Climbing

Summer climbers are not immune from avalanches. Any fresh fall of snow will avalanche off steep slopes either because the old snow provides a good sliding surface or because the new snow had lost its internal cohesion. On the plus side, milder summer temperatures and increased amount of solar radiation greatly speeds up metamorphism and settlement of new snow. In very hot weather or if soaked by rain the old snow surface will soften and peel off in layers as surface slides which can easily cause a climber to loose his footing.

Fig. 1.6 Wet snow sluffs in summer can carry the climber over cliffs or into bergschrunds and crevasses. Photo by Leon Kubbernus.

Fig. 1.7 Returning to base camp with the body of a Sherpa killed in an
avalanche which swept down onto the Khumbu Icefall, Mount Everest.
Photo courtesy of 1982 Canadian Mount Everest Expedition.

Expedition Climbing

In the higher mountain ranges of the world — the Himalaya, the Andes and the high peaks of the Yukon and Alaska — avalanches are a major threat to climbers. They vary in size from small sluffs to some of the largest avalanches known to man; members of the Canadian Expedition to climb Dhaulagiri 4 in winter witnessed an avalanche of monster proportions that fell 3,300 metres from near the summit of Annapurna 2 to the valley floor, then travelled in a boiling cloud of snow dust finally dissipating below the knoll on which the climbers were standing 15 km distant. Unfortunately this type of avalanche is totally unpredictable, an "act of God" if you like, as are the more insidious ice avalanches caused by the collapse of seracs in the relatively fast moving Himalayan icefalls. It's a proven fact that the Khumbu Icefall is the most dangerous section of the normal route up Mount Everest. During the first ascent in 1953, the dangers so impressed themselves upon the expedition members that particularly horrific sections were awarded names like "Atom Bomb" area, "Hell-fire Ally" and "Hillary's Horror". Chris Bonnington in "Everest - South West Face" compares entering these labyrinths of frozen ice to the game of Russian roulette, *"All you can do is to try and pick out a route which is as safe as possible, but there will always be sections which are threatened by ice towers which, sooner or later, must collapse. You just hope that no-one happens to be beneath them when the inevitable collapse occurs."*

Much more predictable are loose snow avalanches which fall almost continually down steep mountainsides after a fresh snowfall. Slab avalanches on lee slopes are much more dangerous because they can occur on relatively shallow slopes which, to the climber, seem the very epitome of security. A slab avalanche killed British climber Nick Estcourt on such a slope on K2 in 1978. Chris Bonnington and Joe Tasker, fixing ropes low down on the mountain between Camp 1 and Camp 2, elected to traverse across a snow slope rather than climb the rock ridge above which looked too difficult and time consuming. The snow slope, steep at first, became so easy angled that no line was fixed across it. Two days of heavy snowfall followed. On the third day the skies cleared but it remained windy. The landscape appeared unchanged, but not quite; the easy-angled slope had been transformed by snow and wind into a death trap. The support party carrying food and gear for Camp 2 found the going very heavy with all the fresh snow, and when they came to the easy angled slope, which had not been fixed, led out a 5 mm cord which was to act as a steadying handrail in the event of surface sluff breaking away under their feet. Doug Scott made it across without incident. It appears that it was Estcourt, the middle man, who triggered the slope which fractured 6' down to the old snow about 100' above their traverse line. He stood no chance. Scott had a lucky escape when the line joining him to Estcourt snapped and stopped his whirlwind descent to certain death.

The size and frequency of Himalayan and Alaskan avalanches often makes the safe placement of camps very difficult. There are a number of reported instances of camps being demolished by windblast from large avalanches even though they were protected from the moving snow.

The problems of avoiding avalanches in these regions are summarized below:

— The short good weather seasons in the eastern Himalaya (pre and post-monsoon) require expeditions to tackle the lower slopes of the mountain in the heavy snowfall periods preceding good weather.

— The short time-scale expeditions face when attempting larger peaks requires continuous pushing of the route despite the conditions.

— The necessity to supply climbers further up the mountain.

— The desire to make progress after periods of inactivity usually caused by fresh snowfall.

— Climbers, used to climbing high-angled slopes, fail to recognize the danger on slopes of lower angle which they consider easy ground.

Waterfall Ice Climbing

Fig 1.8 John Lauchlan on Polar Circus during an earlier ascent. On his solo attempt in 1982, the avalanche released close to the point from which this photograph was taken. Photo by Raymond Jotterand.

Frozen waterfalls form in gully systems or down cliff faces which often have steep talus slopes below the start of the climb and large snow collection areas above. Because difficult ice climbs take several hours, even days to complete, climbers are exposed to possible avalanche hazard for considerable periods of time during which conditions may change for the worse. You've only got to think of the effect of the sun striking the slopes above the climb, a sudden warming trend in the weather, or the additional weight of further snowfall. Near the town of Field in the Canadian Rockies, two climbers were standing below a climb discussing the best line to take when a small avalanche shot over the top of the ice and carried them several metres downhill over boulders and some small cliff bands. More recently four climbers were avalanched off the same waterfall and one of them was buried and died. Although it was cold down in the valley, the sun had been on the upper slopes above the waterfall for some hours.

In another incident during an early ascent of Cascade Waterfall near Banff the leader was left dangling from an ice screw after being swept off the crux by an avalanche from the bowl above.

John Lauchlan, one of Canada's leading mountaineers, was not so lucky. He was attempting the first solo ascent of Polar Circus, a 620 metre high Grade 6 ice climb in the Canadian Rockies, a route he'd climbed in one and a half days four years earlier. He had completed the first two pitches and was climbing a steep snow bowl to get to the foot of the next pitch when the slope fractured just above him and carried him back down the snow slope and over a 20 metre high cliff. Although not buried by the slide he died of injuries suffered in the fall. Later it was perceived from his tracks that John, the most safety conscious of climbers, had recognized the danger and instead of climbing up the middle of the bowl, had been contouring around the top edge in an effort to minimize the risk.

Equipment to Carry

The equipment you need to take on any winter trip naturally depends on the nature of the tour; the length, terrain, season and objectives. Such information, in much greater detail than I have space for, can be found in any good textbook or magazine on ski touring and mountaineering.

There are, however, some items indirectly related to the subject of avalanches that should be stressed. If you are using light cross-country shoes or single boots, the most important survival items are spare socks and insulated canvas overboots. The type of overbootee made for cross-country shoes is useful when travelling in cold weather, but is not sufficient for prolonged stops in the case of an accident. Down or fiberfill jackets can be lifesavers and in very cold weather, especially if children are along, a light-weight sleeping bag in the party is well worth considering.

Some form of equipment repair kit is a must. It is surprising what can be achieved with only a spare ski tip, a length of picture wire and a roll of fiberglass-reinforced tape. A more versatile kit would include screwdriver, pliers, spare screws, spare bindings and basket. Whatever your needs make sure the kit is not so large that you are tempted to leave it behind.

And now let's look at some of the specialized equipment directly related to travel in avalanche country:

Avalanche Rescue Beacons

Avalanche Rescue Beacons, sometimes called Avalanche Transceivers, are electronic devices capable of both transmitting and receiving a radio signal. When travelling in avalanche terrain each person in a party carries one of these devices switched to transmit; because power usage is minimal, they are usually kept switched on all day. If someone gets buried by an avalanche, the rescue beacon will carry on transmitting the signal. Their companions will immediately switch their own units to receive and begin a predetermined search pattern. Typically, if the victim is buried 1 m below the surface and the searchers are 50 m away at the start of the search, it should be possible to dig out the victim in under 10 minutes.

At the present time, there is no doubt that avalanche rescue beacons offer the fastest and most reliable method for locating a buried avalanche victim. Since their introduction in North America they have already been credited with saving lives; they appear to have the potential for increasing the depth at which live recoveries are usually made. They are widely used by professionals engaged in avalanche work—even by rescue dogs—and many ski clubs that conduct serious mountain tours are also buying them. All serious mountain tourers, whether skiers, snowboarders or snowmobilers are urged to buy one, or even two. Loan one to a friend when you go out; it's cheap insurance.

Avalanche Beacon Standards

In the past, avalanche transceivers in North America operated on one of two different frequencies (2275 Hz or 457 kHz). A few years ago North America decided to standardize on the 'European' frequency of 457 kHz. At this time (fall 1998) there are only a few die-hards using the old Skadi, Ramer or Pieps 1 models, which operated at 2275 Hz. There are still quite a few people using dual-frequency models that were manufactured during the transition period, however, as these beacons are phased out the old 2275 Hz units will become useless. Nowadays you can only purchase 457 kHz single frequency tranceivers.

In recent years improvements in transceiver technology have resulted in avalanche beacons that are more reliable, easier to use in all kinds of conditions and reasonably compatible with each other (although, of course, more expensive).

In the past year there has been another major advance in technology with the introduction of the first digital transceiver, the "Tracker". The advantage of digital technology over the old analog technology is that it is now possible to compute and display such facts as how many people are buried, how far away they are, and their direction. It is possible to display step-by-step instructions, a clock to show how long

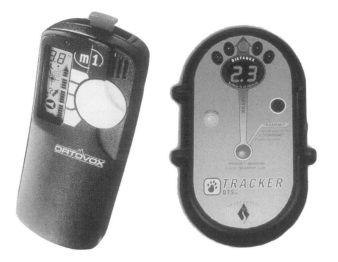

Fig. 1.9 There have been many advances in transceiver technology over the last few years such as audible speakers and LED displays. However, digital transceivers with their computational power and sophisticated displays will allow for a shorter learning curve and faster search times. Stay tuned.

Shown here are the leading Avalanche Rescue Beacons (1998) in the digital technology race. From left to right Ortovox M1 with digital display and the Tracker DTS Digital Avalanche Transceiver.

you have been searching, or any other features a manufacturer might think useful.

The main selling point for the new digital transceiver is that it has a short learning curve and is simple to operate. Testing has shown the Tracker to be much faster than analog receivers when searching for one person in a relatively small slide path. However, there were some compatibility problems due to differing pulse rates (beeps per second) when searching for multiple burials using a mix of transceiver models.

While the Tracker may be the first digital receiver on the market, other models will soon follow, either all digital or a combination of analog technology and digital displays. As digital beacons are introduced, be wary of manufacturers' gimmicks which may add to the complexity (and price) without adding much to the ruggedness and simplicity of use.

So what kind of receiver should you buy? Although digital transceivers are new on the market, they have been thoroughly tested and the major concerns of the avalanche professionals have been addressed. Their promise of faster search times and easier use is very compelling, especially if your companions buy the same model. If you go out with large club groups you should buy the type of receiver used by most of the participants. Compatibility is the main issue in this case.

Look for a unit with a simple, foolproof method of switching on and off, and of switching from transmit to receive. A well designed rescue beacon should be easy to use in the pressure and excitement of a rescue.

However easy a transceiver is to use, it is still important to practise searching at the start of every season.

Care of Avalanche Rescue Beacons

Modern avalanche beacons are sealed in injection moulded plastic cases that are rugged and reasonably moisture proof, although condensation can still be a problem. In spite of the electronics being reliable and well protected, avalanche rescue beacons should be treated with respect.

— Try not to drop them and don't throw them around. If you break the ferrite rod antenna the unit will still beep but the frequency won't be correct and the reception of other signals will be noisy.

— Keep the battery terminals clean. If they become oxidized there will be a high resistance connection between the battery and the electronics resulting in the unit working erratically or not at all.

— Remove the batteries at the end of the season. Make sure you install the new batteries correctly. Most models have a diagram on the outside of the case to guide you.

— Organizations that issue or loan rescue beacons should institute a regular schedule for checking the units.

Practising with Avalanche Rescue Beacons

Organized clubs and groups should arrange practise sessions for their members at the beginning of each ski season. As members acquire units throughout the season hold additional sessions. Because avalanche beacons don't work satisfactorily indoors use your local park or any open ground where you can hide or bury the units. Some people practise near the trailhead before or after a ski trip.

Before burying a unit, make sure it's switched on, placed in a plastic bag and well wrapped in a glove or piece of ensolite to protect it from damage during the digging out. If you intend burying it more than a metre below the surface placing it inside a packsack will give shovellers a little larger area to search for. Using another unit, check before leaving the burial site that the beacon is transmitting. If, for some reason, the unit quits working you have three alternatives: to dig for it (if a large area is trampled down this may take some time), to leave it until the spring melt, or to persuade the local avalanche dog handler that it's a good exercise for his dog.

The whole purpose of practising is to emphasize that an organized, systematic approach is preferable to haphazard wandering. You can demonstrate, by timing recoveries, that the organized approach is the more efficient, and that practise greatly improves speed. Practises can be set up as competitions either with individual searchers or with teams of 2 to 3 persons. Bury 2 or more rescue beacons with various spacings to simulate an accident with multiple victims.

You can set your own standards for efficiency. It could be said that a person is proficient when they can lead a group of three searchers in a search area of 100 x 200 m and recover the buried unit in under 6 minutes.

Refer to "Searching with Avalanche Rescue Beacons" on page 172 for details of search methods.

Fig. 1.10 Practice is essential for fast, efficient searching in a backcountry rescue. Photo by Bob Sandford, courtesy Alberta Mountain Council.

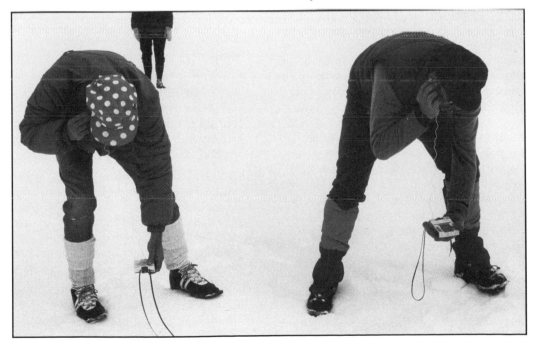

Before a trip Make sure your rescue beacon is working properly and that the batteries are fresh or fully charged. If you are not using rechargeable batteries, use the best alkaline batteries available and change them frequently — you can always use the old batteries in pocket flashlights. And, most important, check that everyone in the group has a compatible unit.

During the trip Rescue beacons should be carried on the person as close to the head as possible. A good procedure is to place the beacon in a shirt pocket with the flap done up. Ensure the beacon's lanyard is about your neck. Some models provide a chest strap to hold the unit tight against your body. Never carry the avalanche beacon in your pack or in the pocket of a garment such as a jacket which you might take off during the day. Keep metal objects such as hardware, knives or radios at least 10 cm away from the avalanche beacon as they will interfere with the signal, decrease the range and reduce battery life. Quartz crystal watches interfere with the signal; take them off.

Switch on your rescue beacon at the start of the day, and leave it on until you are safely encamped or until you have finished the trip. The value of doing this was well illustrated in January 1982 when three Provincial Park Rangers, on their day off, set out on a ski tour in the Healy Creek area of the Canadian Rockies. Out of habit, they switched their beacons to transmit before they left the parking lot. While ascending a small V-shaped valley below treeline, they triggered a small slab avalanche which cleaned off the adjacent side slope right down to the ground, knocking over one of the party in the valley bottom and completely burying him under a metre of snow. Using their avalanche beacons his companions were able to dig him out, shaken but unhurt, within a few minutes. The victim commented later, *"We didn't consider that we were in avalanche terrain where the accident happened. It was a complete surprise"*. The ending might have been very different had they waited until they reached an area considered hazardous before switching on their rescue beacons.

Checking Avalanche Beacons at the Start of a Trip

At the start of each day all avalanche beacons should be checked using the following procedure:

— One member, with his unit on transmit, moves out from the rest of the group and stops only when the remainder of the party, their units switched to receive, can no longer hear the signal.

— The main group now switches their units to transmit, while the person out in front switches to receive.

— In turn, each party member skis towards the checker and carries on past the person until well out of range on the other side.

Summary

There are a few important points concerning the use of avalanche rescue beacons which you should remember:

— Although rescue beacons provide the fastest means of recovering a person from under avalanche debris, they are no guarantee that the victim will be recovered alive. They don't give you a licence to take risks.

— Everyone in the party must be equipped with a compatible unit which is in good working order, is switched on, and has adequate power remaining in the batteries.

— Everyone who uses an avalanche rescue beacon in the back country should practice a few times at the start of every touring season. Practice is the only way you will achieve the speed and expertise needed to effect a quick recovery.

— It's no use locating a buried person quickly with a rescue beacon if it's going to take hours of scrabbling with hands and ski tails to dig him out. Always have at least two shovels in the party; preferably one for every two persons. Also carry at least one and preferably two sectional probes.

The use of avalanche rescue beacons during a rescue is covered in the chapter "Avalanche Rescue" beginning on page 163.

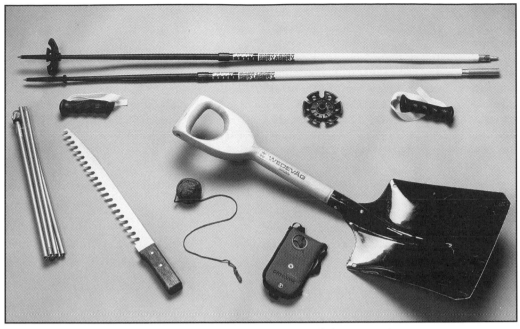

Fig. 1.11 A selection of avalanche safety equipment: probe poles, sectional aluminum probes (too lightweight for professional rescue use, but adequate for backcountry emergencies) snow saw, avalanche cord, rescue beacon and a large snow shovel.

Avalanche Cords

An alternative to avalanche rescue beacons is the avalanche cord, a length of brightly-colored perlon or nylon cord which the skier attaches to himself and trails behind him. Avalanche cords have lost their popularity in recent years due to a controversy about their effectiveness. Some researchers claim that in large avalanches the whole cord is dragged under and remains buried. Nevertheless, there have been instances of people dug out quickly from small slides after being located by their cords. Various ideas such as tying balloons to the end of the cord to keep it above the surface or storing the cord in a container to be deployed when necessary have been tried and found to be impractical.

Avalanche cords are usually 20 m to 30 m long and may be marked at intervals to indicate the direction of and the distance to the buried skier.

Avalanche Probes

The traditional method of locating a buried person is by probing with a steel or aluminum rod. Although avalanche rescue beacons have supplanted probes as the most effective means of locating a victim, probes still have an application in the backcountry. They are not only useful for confirming the precise location after a beacon search, but can also be used for probing for hidden crevasses during glacier travel.

There are two types of probes used today: sectional aluminum tubes 9 mm - 10 mm in diameter which screw together to give any desired length of probe, and ski poles with removable and interchangeable handles and baskets which can be screwed together to give a probe length of 2 to 2.5 metres. Avalanche-probe poles, although expensive when compared with normal ski poles, are highly recommended.

Shovels

A large shovel is essential for the quick digging out of a buried victim. It has been estimated that for a victim buried 1.3 m deep at least 1 cubic metre of snow has to be removed before artificial respiration can be applied. With skis and hands this would take a minimum of 40 minutes in compact debris, whereas with a shovel it would take only about 8 minutes.

Although there are many snow shovels on the market, most are unsatisfactory, being either too flimsy or too small for moving avalanche snow. A large shovel, one which will just fit inside a pack, will move snow at 3 times the rate of a small one. Choose a scoop-sized shovel with a blade strong enough to dig through heavy avalanche snow and a short removable handle with a "D" grip for efficient digging. A good compromise is to buy a cheap hardware store aluminum scoop shovel, knock out the rivet which holds the handle to the scoop and cut down or replace the handle using a wing-nut and bolt for fastening.

Climbing Rope

A climbing rope, preferably a full weight 11 mm rope, can be used for protection when crossing narrow gullies or when kicking snow off from above when descending a steep slope. Because of the large forces involved over a period of several seconds, good belaying techniques must be used. Static belays to trees or rocks should be used if at all possible.

Snow Saw

A snow saw with an aluminum blade and a wooden handle is useful for cutting blocks for igloos or shelter walls and for conducting the Shovel Shear test. See page 103.

Thermometer

Many travellers carry a small thermometer to record the temperature of the air. A thermometer is also useful when studying the snowpack so why not carry one suitable for both purposes? The best type to buy is a small dial-stem thermometer with a protective case which records temperatures ranging from +30 C to -40 C.

Magnifying Glass

When analyzing the stability of the snowpack in some areas you need to know the type of snow crystals in certain layers of the snowpack. For this purpose you should obtain a 8x to 10x magnifying glass. Most photographic stores sell a type with a clear plastic base which can be placed directly onto a crystal screen or other suitable board.

Crystal Screen

If you are interested in measuring the size of snow crystals you need a crystal screen which is a rectangle of either aluminum or plastic material with one or more millimetre grids. Snow crystals are collected on the screen and viewed through a magnifying glass against the background of the grid. Many mountaineering equipment stores are now selling crystal screens.

Inclinometer

Among the more useful gadgets available to the backcountry skier is a simple plastic inclinometer. There are several different models available to help the backcountry powder-hound estimate slope angle to within 2 or 3 degrees. Some compasses have built-in inclinometers.

2

Mountain Weather

Because changes in the snowpack leading to avalanche hazard are greatly influenced by weather, a knowledge of the effects of temperature change, sun, wind, or rain on the snowpack is absolutely essential. It's possible for the back country traveller to decide if avalanche hazard is likely to either increase or decrease by making an intelligent interpretation of present meteorological conditions coupled with a knowledge of past weather.

Skiers and climbers are primarily concerned with **changes** in weather conditions and with the effect of these changes on the old snowpack and on any new snowfall. It is important to remember that a **significant** change in the weather results in a change in the stability of the snowpack. The most important factors to consider are:

— **The amount of snow** and the intensity of the snowfall.

— **Wind speed** and direction of both prevailing and local winds.

— **Temperature changes;** particularly sudden rises in temperature.

The Atmosphere

The earth's atmosphere consists of a mixture of gasses, with Oxygen and Nitrogen making up about 90% of the volume. Other important constituents, as far as weather is concerned, are water vapor, ozone and carbon dioxide — all of which influence the radiation balance — and solid and liquid particles — dust, volcanic ash, tiny droplets of sulfuric or nitric acid, and salt from the sea — called aerosols. Aerosols, which may exist in the mountain atmosphere in concentrations as high as 150,000 particles per cubic centimetre, provide condensation nuclei for precipitation. The atmosphere is bound to the earth by the force of gravity; it has no upper surface, but blends slowly into interplanetary space. The pressure created by the atmosphere is greatest at the surface of the earth, and decreases with altitude. The usual measure of atmospheric pressure is the millibar, (mb) which is approximately 1000th of the atmospheric pressure at sea level. Sea level is usually considered to average 1013 mb while the 500 mb pressure level is at approximately 5000 m (18,000'). The lower atmosphere, in which most of our weather phenomena occurs, and which contains most of the water vapor, is called the Troposphere.

Transfer of heat from the ground to the air and the evaporation and condensation of water involving latent heat creates an atmosphere which is constantly on the move transporting heat, moisture and momentum in the form of winds. The circulation pattern is further complicated by the earths rotation on its axis which gives an apparent deflection to air which would normally circulate directly between areas of high and low pressure.

Because atmospheric gasses expand and contract as pressure changes, the density of the atmosphere varies with pressure. When air is heated it expands causing the density to decrease. In order to establish equilibrium, the warmer air, which is lighter than its surroundings, rises. Similarly, air which is cooled may become dense compared

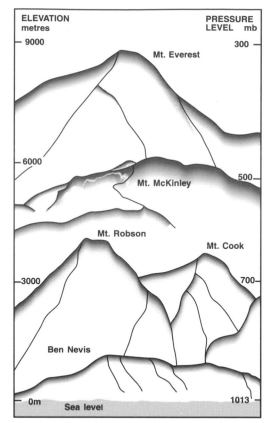

Fig. 2.2 Decrease of pressure with elevation. At the 500 mb level airflow is free from friction with the earth's surface except where it passes over high mountain ranges.

with its surroundings and tend to sink. Thus, low level warm air will replace high level cold air and vice versa.

Particularly applicable to precipitation is the fact that the temperature of a rising mass of air tends to fall as the air mass rises because, as atmospheric pressure decreases with altitude so the air expands, and like the air escaping from an inflated tire it cools.

At this stage we must differentiate between air flow at different altitudes. At the 500 mb (5000 m) level the air flow is relatively free from friction with the earths surface, except where it passes over high mountain ranges. These are called prevailing winds. At lower elevations, friction and terrain features have considerable effect on the air flow and give rise to secondary pressure systems below the main circulation which result in local wind systems.

Weather Patterns Producing Snow

Moisture, in the form of water vapor, must be present in the atmosphere for any appreciable amount of snow to fall. Most of the moisture providing snowfall on the western mountains of North America comes from the Pacific Ocean. As moist air is swept in over the Pacific Ocean as a result of the low pressure area which frequently develops over the Gulf of Alaska in winter, it produces heavy snowfalls in the Pacific North-west and the Coast Ranges of British Columbia. Farther south, major storms tracking in across the Pacific from the west and south-west give rise to heavy precipitation in the Sierras. Warm moist air from the Gulf of Mexico meeting cold Arctic air may result in heavy snowfalls on the east slopes of the Colorado Rockies. Inland, the amount of moisture available decreases rapidly and only the higher, steeper ranges such as the Selkirks and the Rockies receive any large amounts of snow. The foothills of the Canadian Rockies tend to receive the most snow from north-easterly winds which blow when an Arctic high is over the Yukon and a low pressure area is over Montana. The European mountains depend upon the Atlantic depressions for most of their snowfall. Ranges close to the ocean such as the Pyrenees suffer from unpredictable weather with heavy snowfalls and variable temperatures. Farther east conditions are more predictable; snowfalls are lighter and drier. In the central and eastern Alps long periods of fine weather may be encountered in winter when a great high pressure area sits over northern Europe. The mountains of Scotland, have the unpredictable weather and rapid changes of temperature associated with ranges close to the ocean, but because of their modest elevation are not subject to extreme snowfalls; they receive the majority of their precipitation as rain. The New Zealand Alps are a wall of high peaks rising from the ocean. North-west winds bring warm moist air from the Tasman Sea giving heavy snowfall and the most unpredictable weather of any popular mountain range

The Lifting of Moist Air

There are three important ways in which molecules of water vapor rise and produce snow. They are Orographic Lifting, Cyclonic Lifting, and Frontal Lifting.

Orographic lifting is by far the most important lifting mechanism in the production of severe, avalanche-producing storms in the western mountains of Canada and the U.S.A. As horizontally-moving air masses are forced over mountain ranges they rise, and cool rapidly. The rate of lifting is ten times greater than that of Cyclonic or Frontal Lifting. It was mentioned earlier that the amount of precipitation depends upon the moisture content of the air and the rate at which it is lifted. In turn the rate of lifting depends upon the wind speed, the slope of the mountain barrier and how close to a right angle the wind hits the mountain range. Most of the snowfall in the Coast Ranges is caused by the orographic lifting of moist air from the Pacific Ocean. Further inland there is less moisture in the air, the cloud layers tend to be thinner and so the amount of precipitation is reduced.

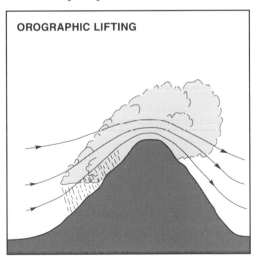

OROGRAPHIC LIFTING

Fig. 2.3 Lifting of moist air over high mountain ranges. Because the air stops rising, the condensation level is higher on the lee slopes.

Cyclonic lifting is the lifting of large air masses as the result of the general circulation pattern of the atmosphere. These air masses, or cyclones, are the areas of low pressure seen on the weather maps and may range in diameter from 100 km to 3000 km. In the northern hemisphere the air circulates in an anti-clockwise direction around these low pressure centres. In temperate latitudes cyclones produce much of the winter precipitation, though in mountainous area they may be substantially modified by the terrain. In the absence of mountain barriers, the rate of lifting is rarely more than a few centimetres per second and the weather over areas dominated by cyclones is usually uniformly cloudy with moderate precipitation.

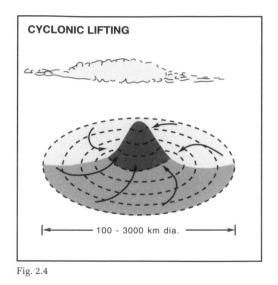

Fig. 2.4

Frontal lifting. The masses of air circulating around an area of low pressure have often come from different geographical regions, and as a result there may exist sharp transition zones separating cold dry air such as the Continental Arctic air mass from warmer moister air of the prevailing westerlies. The boundary where two air masses meet is called a front. Because the cold air is denser, the warm air mass will always ride up over the cold air, and in the process of lifting often produces precipitation. The area where the warm air advances and pushes up over the cold air is known as a **Warm Front**, while the steeper **Cold Front** is formed when the cold air pushes its way below warm air. As the system decays, the cold front begins to overtake the warm front in a process called occlusion which results in an **Occluded Front**. The principal frontal system in the atmosphere is the **"Arctic Front"** where cold arctic air and warmer tropical air meet.

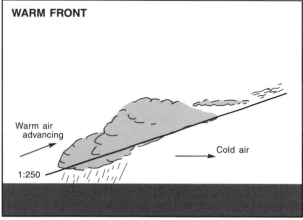

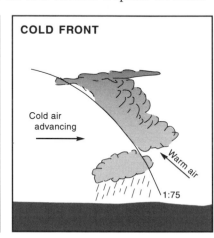

Fig. 2.5

36

Snowfall

The depth of snowfall at any location is influenced by the amount of moisture present in the air and the speed at which it rises. The warmer the air, the more moisture it can carry; the faster it rises, the greater the intensity of snowfall. The rate of lifting depends on the steepness of the mountain range together with wind speed and direction. Maximum snowfall occurs when a mountain range is at right angles to the moisture-laden winds.

It is important when considering the deposition of snow to differentiate between mountain ranges which confront major weather systems and smaller areas where deposition is dependent upon local wind patterns. Local winds may denude the windward side of a mountain where one would have expected the greater amount of snow to have fallen, and conversely, deposit snow on localized lee slopes.

The warmer the air the more moisture it can hold. This results in a tendency for greater snowfalls from storms which originate in warmer areas such as the Pacific Ocean than from storms which originate in Continental Polar regions.

Snowfall Intensity

The rate at which snow falls, and the precipitation intensity, has a direct bearing on the development of avalanche hazard. High rates of snowfall — 2 cm/h or greater, especially when accompanied by wind — are usually responsible for major periods of direct-action avalanche activity. While the critical amounts vary from region to region, any heavy, intense snowfall of several hours duration should be considered potentially hazardous from the skier's point of view.

How Snowfall is Measured

Snowfall can be measured and recorded in several different ways depending on how the results are to be used. Depth of new snow is useful for establishing how fast the snow is settling, while the intensity of snowfall is an indicator of how fast avalanche slopes are being loaded with new snow. An even better indicator of loading is the precipitation intensity as it does not depend on the density of the snow. A summary of measurements commonly used with units and typical values are given below. These values will be less for drier interior ranges and greater for coastal ranges.

Measuring Snowfall	
Term used	Units
Snow depth	10 cm of snow
Snowfall rate	1 cm of snow per hour
Water equivalent	10 mm of water

Forecasting Snowfall

Hazard from direct-action avalanches is directly related to the amount and intensity of snowfall. For this reason, forecasts of snowfall amounts are important in areas where direct-action avalanches are a source of danger. In the past few years, with the advent of high speed computers, attempts have been made, quite successfully, in both the U.S.A. and Canada to provide accurate snowfall predictions for selected areas.

Most impressive is the Colorado Avalanche Warning Program. Maps showing the usual deposition of precipitation throughout Colorado for every 30 of wind direction are used along with daily meteorological reports sent from about 60 stations in the mountains in predicting new snow depths and rate of snowfall. The end result is a rating of potential hazard for various mountain areas.

Increase of Snowfall with Altitude

It's common knowledge that in the lower ranges such as the European Alps and the North American mountains snowfall is greater at higher elevations. Why?

As moist air rises it cools due both to expansion and to the decrease of temperature with altitude. The cooler air cannot hold as much moisture so condensation occurs. If the condensation level is below the freezing point snow will fall. Maximum precipitation occurs just at the base of the clouds where there is maximum moisture and maximum condensation.

Over a period of time, the amount of moisture in an air mass is reduced, the condensation level rises and precipitation only occurs when the air is forced up to higher elevations. This process, which on an average results in higher elevations getting a larger share of the available moisture, continues until either all the moisture has been used up, or the moist air stops rising and passes over the range.

Maximum precipitation occurs just to the windward side of the range. This is probably due to the shape of the airflow as it crosses a mountain barrier, the lines of flow flattening out before the summit ridge. Once past the summit there is no more lifting and so little precipitation.

Fig. 2.6 Wind-drifted snow in the Canadian Rockies. Photo by Bob Sandford, courtesy Alberta Mountain Council.

Wind

It is the subtle, eddying wind gently depositing snow in insignificant hollows which makes the small but deadly slab avalanche. It is the wind, blowing hard across mountain ridges which builds up treacherous cornices — the natural trigger of many a slide. It is the wind gusting across mountainsides which moves and shapes the snow into gentle rounded slabs so deceptively attractive to the downhill powder-hound. Wind plays a most important part in the development of hazardous avalanche conditions. The mountain traveller must understand how wind transports and deposits snow, and be able to recognize from ground features the results of wind deposition.

Prevailing Winds

These are the winds which predominate in a particular area; the high level winds which, as part of the main circulation, are responsible for the overall weather pattern. There may be one or more prevailing wind directions in any geographical area. For instance, in western Canada, southwest winds bring snowfall to the mountains and Chinooks to the easterly plains, while southerly winds often herald fine, dry weather. These winds are usually well defined and form the basis for long range meteorological predictions.

Local Winds

Local winds are much more unpredictable and depend on prevailing winds, terrain features, temperature and even the time of day. For information on local wind direction, the traveller must depend on observation in the field; one aspect of avalanche prediction where the tourer has an advantage over the desk-bound hazard forecaster who has to rely on meteorological forecasts and remote weather stations for his information.

Fig. 2.7 Prevailing winds are high-level winds blowing across mountain ranges. Closer to the ground, where wind direction is modified by terrain, local winds often blow parallel to the valleys.

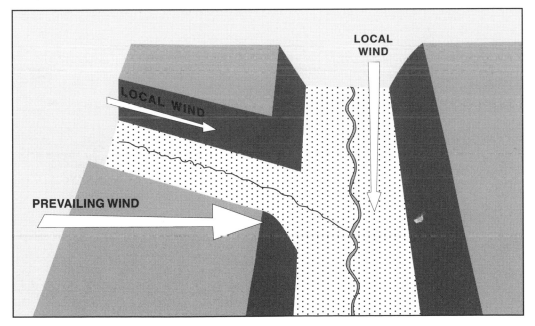

How Wind Transports Snow

Wind speed across a mountain side varies as the wind passes over or between various terrain features. Snow is picked up where the wind is steady or where it accelerates and is dropped where the wind slows down. The amount of snow transported depends on the wind speed, the type of snow crystals and the looseness of the snow cover. Cold new snow is readily transported by moderate winds whereas little snow will be removed from an old settled snow surface.

Light winds tend to deposit falling snow on the windward side of trees and rocks, especially if the snow is wet. Over the mountains an even blanket of snow is deposited with a tendency for slightly greater deposition on the windward side.

As the wind increases above 5 km/hr, so the movement of snow begins. At first, activity is confined to the few millimetres above the snow surface as snow particles are rolled along by the wind. Little snow is actually transported in this manner although the resulting rearrangement of snow crystals contributes to the toughness of the snow due to joining of the more closely packed grains.

Medium wind speeds will begin to pick the snow up off the ground and bounce the crystals along the surface. The airstream at this stage is still uniform and steady and most of the activity is confined to the first few centimetres above the snow surface. Although the wind is only of moderate strength, a considerable quantity of snow can be transported and loaded onto lee slopes and the lee sides of ridges to form extensive deposits of slab. Poles standing three metres clear of the snow surface on the headwall of Coire Cas in the Cairngorms of Scotland were completely buried during a snowfall of 15 cm accompanied by winds of 70 km/hr and in Colorado snow deposition rates as high as 45 cm/hr have been measured.

As the velocity of the wind increases so does its snow-carrying capacity. Each time the wind speed doubles, the amount of snow it can carry increases by a factor of eight. At a certain velocity, depending on the terrain and the roughness of the snow surface, the wind no longer flows steadily over the snow but becomes turbulent. Turbulence is an uneven air flow which produces eddies or vortices both vertically and horizontally. These eddies do not occur in one location but are continually moving, building up and dying down, producing an extremely complex pattern of air currents at the snow surface. Strong eddies will create a scouring action in the snow and cause erosion. An example of this are scour holes around trees and buildings. Where wind speeds are moderate, snow is usually deposited by the eddies. Snow fences rely on eddies reducing the wind speed behind the fence to create snowdrifts. In turbulent air conditions snow particles are held in suspension, by upward air currents, from a few centimetres above the snow surface to a considerable height. Very large volumes of snow may be transported in this manner.

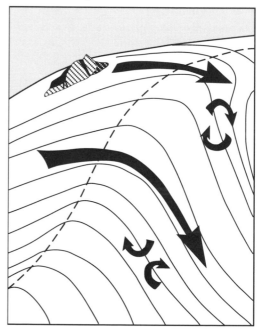

Fig. 2.8 Eddies, or vortices, formed on the lee side of any windbreak are responsible for the deposition and packing of snow into cohesive slabs.

Effect of wind on snow crystals

Modification of snow crystals both in the atmosphere and after they reach the ground is an important factor in the development of avalanche hazard.

High winds will cause crystal collisions in the atmosphere, breaking up the more delicate forms such as stellar crystals into smaller fragments. On reaching the ground crystals may be dragged along the surface, bounced off the terrain or picked up and swirled around several metres above the surface before finally being deposited. High wind speeds — 90 km/hr or more — will scour the snow, reducing the size of cornices and etching the windward side of drifts.

Wind blown snow tends to be tougher, more closely knit, denser and more cohesive. Snow deposited by high winds loses its crystalline characteristics and appears duller — hard slab is often described as chalky white in appearance. As a general rule wind-carved snow formations are usually safe while snow deposited by wind is often unsafe.

Way in which Wind Creates Cohesive Slabs

The exact mechanism by which cohesive slabs are created is not fully understood. There is no doubt that wind plays an important part in slab formation, although I have seen direct action slab avalanches in the Yukon during and shortly after an apparently windless, but heavy snowstorm. It is also thought that high humidity enhances slab formation as snow particles remain in suspension in the air for longer distances without subliming when the humidity is high. High humidity also allows a greater build-up of rime on the individual crystals.

Two actions of the wind appear to help in forming slabs. First of all, wind breaks up the more delicate crystals into smaller particles — as small as 0.1 mm — and second, the action of the wind physically packs the snow crystals closer together. Because individual snow crystals tend to be broken into small particles the snow becomes small grained and more rounded. Because of greater sintering due to close grain contact, the snow is stronger for a given density.

Deposition of Slabs and Cushions

The greatest danger to the skier is from either direct or delayed action slab avalanches. Such slabs are deposited by local winds according to wind direction and terrain features. Certain terrain features enhance the formation of slabs.

Think of air flowing over a bare, rounded ridge (Fig. 2.9). The wind is approaching the ridge at a uniform speed and at a constant pressure. Because of pressure restraints, the same amount of air is forced through a narrower space at the top of the ridge with the result that the air on the windward side is forced to accelerate, reaching maximum velocity at the crest of the ridge. Snow on the higher windward slope will be picked up by the accelerating wind thus denuding the windward side of snow. Once over the ridge the air can expand downwards which has the effect of reducing the wind velocity. The reduction in wind speed allows the snow which has been carried over the ridge to be deposited. Because flow over rounded ridges is often a steady flow and cornices do not form, other signs must be used to determine wind direction.

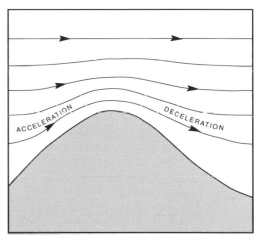

Fig. 2.9 Airflow over a rounded ridge.

41

As the ridge becomes sharper, so the accelerating and decelerating effect of the wind is intensified to such an extent that eventually the flow on the lee side of the ridge is turbulent with accompanying vortices or circular swirls. In moderate wind speeds of around 25 km/hr, cornices begin to form (Fig. 2.10). As more snow is transported over the ridge the cornice grows and may eventually overhang the lee side of the ridge with many tonnes of snow. Cornices overhanging steep lee slopes are often very unstable due to lack of support. In the long run high winds tend to erode a cornice reducing its size. Sometimes a mound of soft slab called a snow cushion forms immediately below a cornice; in some cases the whole slope is covered in soft slab. These cushions are extremely dangerous during and shortly after formation.

Some of the most subtle and insidious deposits of soft slab occur below changes in terrain steepness (Fig. 2.11) and it is these small areas of slab which can so easily catch the skier unaware. Note how succeeding layers of snow steepen up the slope and how the potential fracture line moves down the slope as the season progresses. Large areas of relatively flat terrain above such a slope can be the source of a considerable amount of snow during fair weather drifting.

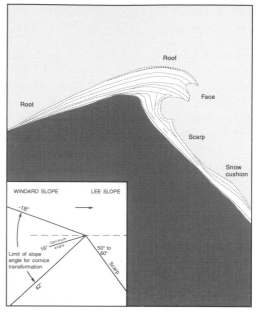

Fig. 2.10 The buildup of a cornice showing the critical angle of the windward slope for cornice formation. The maximum angle of the scarp is approximately 60°.

Fig. 2.11 Relatively small changes in terrain steepness may develop dangerously soft slabs. See Figs. 4.13 and 9.3

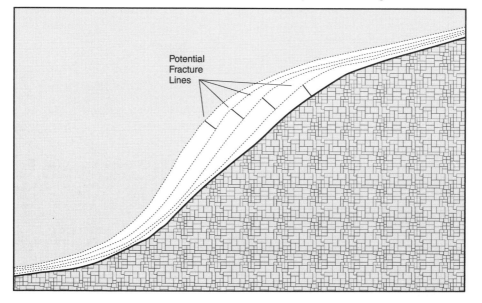

Notches or cols in mountain ridges are natural avenues for the wind, the terrain again accelerating the wind as it passes over the col and slowing it down on the other side where areas of slab are then deposited. Often prevailing winds will blow over the gap while at the same time local winds, blowing at an angle along the mountain side, distort the deposition pattern (Fig. 2.12).

In the mountains local winds often blow along valleys rather than across them, irrespective of the direction of the prevailing winds. When valley winds blow across a series of mountain ridges they will pick up snow on the windward side and deposit it on the lee side (Fig. 2.13). Higher wind speeds, usually above treeline, will deposit smaller areas of hard slab in isolated pockets.

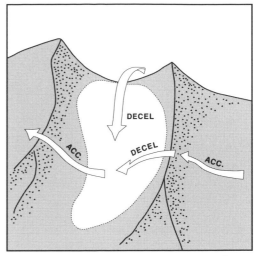

Fig. 2.12 Effect of wind across a mountain side and across a gap in a ridge. After the Avalanche Handbook.

Fig. 2.13 Wind blowing down the valley has created wind-blown ridges and slab-filled channels along the side of Dolomite Peak in the Canadian Rockies.

Difference Between Windslab and Windcrust

Many tourers have difficulty distinguishing between snow which has been shaped by wind such as wind-rippled snow and sastrugi which are usually safe, and wind-deposited snow such as cushions and slabs which are often unsafe. They often find it difficult to decide whether they are on windcrust or windslab, especially if there is a layer of fresh snow on top.

The major difference between slab and crust, and one which indicates whether or not the slope is safe, is that slab has little bonding to the layer underneath, while crust is more firmly attached to the underlayers.

The second basic difference is the aspect of the slope. Slab is found mainly on lee slopes and windcrust on exposed windward slopes. Due to the vagaries of eddying wind currents however, slab has sometimes been found on ridge crests where one would not normally expect to see it.

Windcrust often shows wind rippling or etching; slabs nearly always have a characteristic smooth rounded appearance. Both forms break up into blocks, but whereas slabs often settle with an ominous "whumph" noise and crack over a large area, crust will break underfoot only as you pass over it.

Mountain Winds

Certain wind patterns peculiar to mountain regions influence the snowpack:

Katabatic Winds Air lying over an elevated plateau area such as a glacier or icefield will become denser due to cooling by long wave radiation on a cold, clear night. This denser air will then drain down the mountain slopes and into the valleys below. These Katabatic winds are usually gentle breezes of 15 to 20 km/hr.

In some locations, however, where the air is cooled as it moves across a large snowfield and then drains down through narrow, constricted valleys it can reach very high speeds. This normally occurs along the coasts of Alaska, Greenland and Norway and off some of the worlds larger icefields.

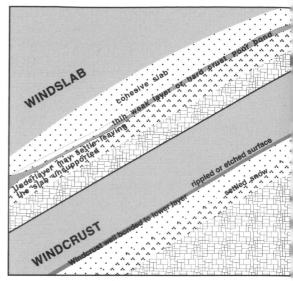

Fig. 2.14 A comparison between windslab and windcrust.

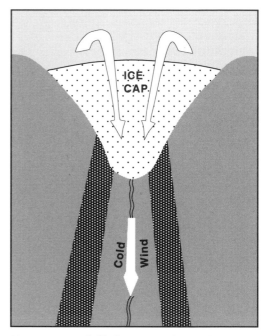

Fig. 2.15 Air, cooled by long-wave radiation, drains down the mountain side into the valley below.

In parts of the world where these winds are especially severe they have been given local names such as the Bora, which brings down cold air from the Austrian Alps to the warmer Adriatic or the Mistral which sweeps down from the French Alps to the Mediterranean.

Chinook and Foehn The Chinook, and its European counterpart the Foehn, are both warm dry winds blowing on the lee side of mountain ranges. The Chinook, which blows over the plains to the east of the Rocky Mountains in Canada and the United States, was named by early settlers who thought the wind originated in Indian territory of that name. The Indians themselves called the wind the "Snow eater" because of the startling way in which large amounts of snow can be evaporated by the warmth and dryness of the air. In addition to warming the air as it passes over the range, Chinook winds also push back the cold arctic air, thus allowing a substantial rise in temperature. The Chinook arch cloud marks the meeting of warm and cold air.

Chinooks are caused when prevailing winds carrying warm, moist air are directed against a mountain range. The forced ascent on the windward side causes clouds to form often with resulting snowfall. During most of the ascent the air is cooled at the moist adiabatic rate of 6°C/km and by the time the air reaches the mountain top much of the moisture will have been removed.

The term adiabatic is used to describe the twin phenomena of decrease in temperature due to expansion of air and increase in temperature due to contraction of air. At the moist adiabatic rate, moisture changes phase — vapor to liquid — due to condensation or alternatively liquid to vapor due to evaporation. Latent heat — the number of calories released or used during condensation or evaporation — either heats or cools the air.

Condensation of moisture in order to give rain or snow releases latent heat which is absorbed by the rising air over the mountain range. As the air descends the lee slope it is warmed at the dry adiabatic rate of 10°C/km so that when the air reaches the bottom of the mountain it is both warmer and drier than the air on the windward side.

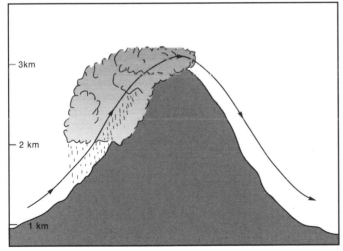
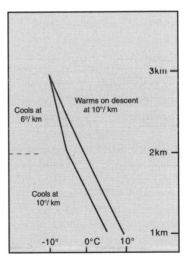

Fig. 2.16 In addition to warming the air as it passes over the range, Chinook winds also push back the cold arctic air, thus allowing a substantial rise in temperature.

Temperature of the Snowpack

The temperature of the snowpack and snow surface changes as heat is transferred within the snowpack and between the snow surface and the air above. Changes in temperature and difference in temperature between layers has a considerable influence on the snowpack's character. Snow exists close to its melting point and any small changes in temperature will affect the strength of the snow and hence its stability. There are three possible areas where heat exchange can take place — the snow surface, the interior of the snowpack and the ground surface.

Heat Transfer at the Snow Surface

Heat may be transferred at the snow surface by conduction, convection, radiation, condensation or evaporation, and precipitation. Often two or more of these processes are present at the same time making the measuring of snow surface temperature a complex problem. This is the reason why experienced cross-country skiers rely on the feel of the snow in their hand rather than a reading from a thermometer when waxing.

Conduction and Convection combine to transfer heat to or from the surface of the snow. The rate of heat transfer is increased in windy conditions. If the wind is both moist and warmer than the snow, heat will be transferred to the snowpack; the higher the wind speed the greater the amount of heat transferred. On the other hand, if cold Arctic air blows across the surface, the snowpack will loose heat to the air and, because of the added effect of evaporation, will cool rapidly and become colder than the air above.

Evaporation and condensation are the source of large exchanges of heat at the snow surface. It requires 600 calories to convert 1 gram of liquid water to vapor without a change in temperature. To convert 1 gram of ice directly to vapor (sublimation) requires 680 calories so you can see that a large quantity of heat, usually provided by strong, warm dry winds, is required to evaporate moisture from the snow surface. Disappointed skiers on the eastern slopes of the Rockies will attest to the phenomenal ability of a Chinook to remove snow. Relatively little evaporation takes place in the absence of wind.

It follows that condensation of water vapor directly on the snow surface will release 680 calories of latent heat to the snow. In this case there must be an excess of water vapor present in the atmosphere. During the formation of surface hoar it is this additional heat which keeps the temperature difference between the snow surface and the air above high enough to allow the continued growth of surface hoar crystals.

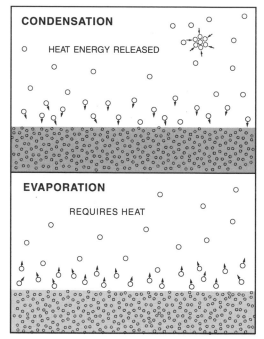

Fig. 2.17 Heat gain and loss due to condensation and evaporation.

Radiation. The amount of incoming solar radiation which reaches the earth is dependent upon the seasons, the latitude and the aspect of the surface relative to the sun's rays. In northern latitudes, north facing slopes receive little or no solar radiation in winter. Areas closer to the poles receive no direct radiation at all during the winter months and even on clear days the snow will loose heat to the atmosphere.

While the atmosphere is virtually transparent to light radiation from the sun, it is relatively opaque to heat radiation from the earth so only a small percentage of the radiated heat is lost to space; the remainder is absorbed by the cloud cover or by the lower layers of the atmosphere.

Snow is an excellent radiator of long-wave radiation. In fact, it is one of the best "blackbody" radiators known. A blackbody radiator refers to a material capable of giving off the maximum amount of radiation at a given temperature. On a clear night, snow may emit enough long-wave radiation to cool the surface by 15°C to 20°C or more. Many climbers have suffered frostbitten feet due to snow cooled in this manner. On a cloudy night, if the atmosphere below the clouds is warmer than the snow, the snow will gain heat.

In the daytime, new snow reflects 80-90% of the short-wave radiation falling on it, so that even on a clear sunny day the snow can still loose heat to the atmosphere from an excess of long-wave radiation. This is one reason why the sparkling layer of surface hoar formed during a clear, calm night will persist unchanged through clear cold weather.

In the spring, the snow becomes less reflective due to melting and dust on the surface, and with the sun higher in the sky the process is reversed and incoming short-wave radiation exceeds the long-wave radiation from the snow surface. The maximum warming from radiation usually occurs with a partially cloudy sky where solar radiation and long-wave radiation from warm clouds combine in the most efficient manner.

Because a large portion of the available short-wave radiation is required to melt the snowpack, air temperatures do not rise significantly in an area until all the new snow has melted.

Fig. 2.18 Average energy balance at the earth's surface. At higher latitudes heat loss exceeds heat gain during the winter months.

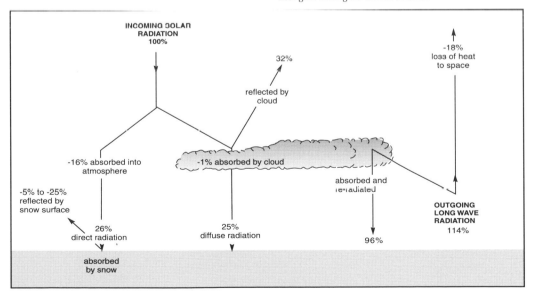

INCOMING SOLAR RADIATION 100%

32% reflected by cloud

-18% loss of heat to space

-16% absorbed into atmosphere

-1% absorbed by cloud

-5% to -25% reflected by snow surface

absorbed and re-radiated

26% direct radiation

25% diffuse radiation

OUTGOING LONG WAVE RADIATION 114%

96%

absorbed by snow

Precipitation. Rain in small quantities contributes little to the transfer of heat at the snow surface. Because it requires 80 calories to convert 1 gram of ice to 1 gram of water without a change temperature, large quantities of warm rain are required before melting at the surface occurs.

Heat Transfer at the Ground Surface

The amount of heat transferred to the snow from the ground is also small. Heat stored within the surface ground layers after the summer months may affect initial snowfalls as the earth gives off enough heat to melt about 1 cm of snow a year. In temperate climates the main effect of the earth's heat is to keep the ground surface temperature from falling much below 0°C.

Heat Transfer Within the Snowpack

Conduction, the transmittal of heat through grain-to-grain contact is the primary mechanism for transmitting heat through the snowpack. The rate of transmission depends on snow structure, density, and depth.

In dry snow conditions very little heat is transferred within the snowpack. This is one of the reasons why such large temperature differences can be found between various layers. Some heat transfer occurs due to sublimation and to circulation of water vapor through the pore spaces.

Conversely heat may be transferred very quickly in the wet snowpack when meltwater or rain percolates through the snow cover. Free water within the snowpack quickly raises the overall temperature to freezing point even though the rain will cause little actual melting. Water, freezing within the snowpack, releases 80 calories of heat per gram to the snowpack.

Fig. 2.19 Modes of heat gain and loss at the snow surface, within the snowpack, and at the ground surface.

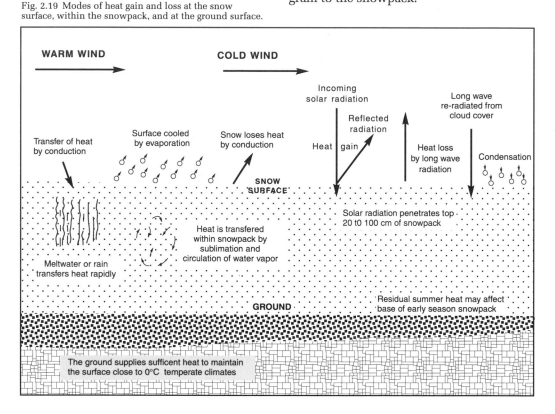

Decrease of Temperature with Height

Within the lower atmosphere, which varies in thickness from about 9 km above the poles to 16 km above the tropics, there is normally a gradual decrease in temperature of approximately 6.5°C for every 1000 m of height gain. Do not confuse this decrease in temperature with the temperature changes associated with rising parcels of air. The dry adiabatic rate for rising air is 10°C/1000 m.

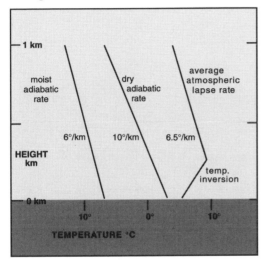

Fig. 2.20 Atmospheric lapse rate.

Temperature Inversions

Temperature inversions occur when the air temperature increases with height above the ground. They occur over a wide range of climatological scales from inversions in the first few millimetres above the snow surface to large scale differences in airmass temperature and can produce dramatic variations in local snow stability within an area.

When the snow surface has been loosing heat due to long-wave radiation, temperature differences as high as 6°C have been measured between the snow surface and the air only 1 mm above. As any winter camper who digs a hole in the snow for his tent will find out, cold air settles in hollows during the course of a still night. Sleeping platforms in igloos and snow caves trap warm air in the top of the structure while cold air settles in the doorway well.

U-shaped mountain valleys are often subject to temperature inversions. On a cold clear night the earth's surface cools by radiating out more heat than it receives; the heavier, colder air near the cooling ground surface sinking to the valley floor. A common indicator of this condition is the cloud or fog layer which sometimes forms at the junction of cold and warm air. If the valley is below treeline you'll notice that the heavily frosted trees low down the slopes give way to trees with no sign of frost at a very well marked demarcation line.

Large scale temperature inversions occur when warm dry air tries to displace a previously well established Continental Arctic air mass. Like the establishment of a warm front, the warm air pushing up over the colder air mass results in much warmer temperatures at higher elevations. Most skiers have had the experience of skiing at 2000 m in -5°C sunshine while the temperature at lower elevations has been -20°C or less.

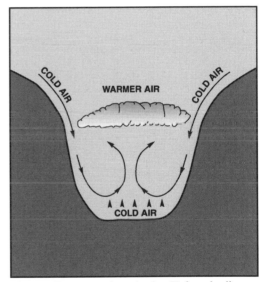

Fig. 2.21 Temperature inversion in a U-shaped valley. Cold air drains down the mountainside and builds up in the valley bottom. The warmest point is at the base of the cloud layer.

3

Snow

Travelling above snow line in winter and summer has many attractions: the tranquility of the frozen landscape, the dazzling whiteness of high alpine snowfields, the almost tangible silence when fresh snowfalls blanket forest and meadows.

Snow can hasten or hinder your progress. In good snow conditions, it's possible to ski many kilometres a day; in poor conditions of crust or rotten snow, progress is frustratingly slow. Firm well consolidated snow allows an easy ascent of steep mountain slopes; loose snow in gullies is a major danger of winter mountaineering. A metre of unconsolidated powder, while enticingly beautiful, creates impossible trail breaking for those on foot.

The shape of snow crystals and their temperature influences how well your skis glide and how well your climbing waxes hold. Safety from avalanches depends upon a countless number of minute physical changes which begin from the first moment the snowflake touches the ground.

It is important when evaluating avalanche hazard and slope stability to consider the various forms of snow, how snow changes on its way to the ground and how the snow-cover builds up in successive layers during the course of the season.

Fig. 3.1 A sparkling layer of surface hoar covers the snow surface hiding the intricate changes which take place in the snowpack below. Photo by Leon Kubbernus.

The Three States of Water

If you want to learn more about how snow forms in the atmosphere and how it changes on the ground read the following section which explains the basic physical concepts governing the three states of water: gas, liquid and solid (vapor, water and ice). Otherwise, turn over the page and resume reading at "Snow in the Air".

Water vapor

Think of water vapor as individual molecules of water dashing around the atmosphere in a state of rapid but random motion. Each molecule consists of one blob of Oxygen with two 'eyes' of Hydrogen attached.

Dew Point

Imagine a large number of molecules of water vapor floating along quite happily in their own cubic centimetre or so of air space. As they are propelled by the prevailing wind landward over the ocean, more molecules freed by evaporation rise up to join them. Eventually they reach land and are swept upwards over high ground. As they rise the air expands and the molecules slow down, their kinetic energy reduced. The more the air expands the cooler the molecules become and the closer together they huddle, until at a certain temperature known as the **Dew Point** they condense into water droplets.

When this occurs the air is said to be **Saturated**. It contains as many free molecules as it possibly can at that particular temperature. The lower the temperature the fewer molecules the air can hold before condensation takes place.

Water

Water is formed of molecules sliding over each other but held together at the same time in a loose liquid form by the attraction of one molecule to another. Because water molecules form strong bonds, a very large amount of energy is required to convert water to vapor. In fact, the evaporation of water requires approximately 540 calories to change 1 gram of water to vapor without a change of temperature. This is known as the Latent Heat of Vaporization. Conversely, condensation releases the equivalent amount of heat to the atmosphere.

Supercooled Water

If water vapor molecules encounter a temperature below freezing before they condense, the clouds which form will be composed of minute droplets which remain in the liquid state below the freezing point. The purer the water the more the droplets can be cooled. But there is a lower temperature limit; at -40°C water droplets freeze instantly.

Vapor Pressure

Some molecules attain enough speed to break away from the surface of water. The higher the temperature the more active the molecules and the greater the evaporation. Many of the molecules which break free remain in the form of an atmosphere of free-moving molecules hovering over the surface of the water. A concentration of these molecules is called Vapor Pressure. As the temperature falls the vapor pressure becomes lower.

Ice

Ice is a state of matter where the molecules are firmly joined and their movement is restricted to vibrations. However, just as in the case of water molecules they are able to break away from surface of the ice and form an atmosphere of vapor.

Vapor Pressure over Water and Ice

For a given temperature below freezing the vapor pressure over water is greater than the vapor pressure over ice. This is because the molecules are able to escape more readily from the water than from the ice. This concept, and the concept of Supersaturation, are most important in the formation of ice crystals both in the atmosphere and on the ground.

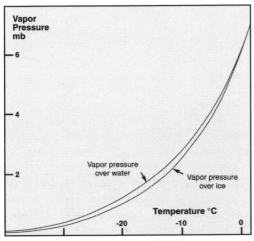

Fig. 3.2 Saturation vapor pressure is higher over ice than over supercooled water.

Condensation

Condensation happens when a large number of molecules join together to form a water droplet. If there is no foreign surface on which to condense, the molecules can only come together by accidental collisions which may require a high degree of Supersaturation especially in the case of slower moving molecules at lower temperatures. If a sufficient number of molecules get together then the droplet will continue to grow rather than evaporate away. In the atmosphere this is achieved by the presence of foreign particles such as dust and salts called Condensation Nuclei, which provide a surface on which water molecules can begin to condense.

Supersaturation

Consider a glass of iced water. If the humidity is high enough it will soon become coated on the outside with condensed water droplets. Like the molecules around the cold glass, high flying molecules in the atmosphere need some surface on which they can begin to condense. In the absence of such a surface, in the very clean air conditions at higher altitudes, it is possible for many more molecules to crowd together before condensation occurs. This higher moisture content is called Supersaturation.

Sublimation

Sublimation is the ability of water molecules to change from ice to vapor and back again without passing through the water stage. A warm dry wind blowing over an ice surface will carry off water molecules and because the vapor pressure over the ice is momentarily lower, more molecules will be encouraged to break away from the surface thus hastening evaporation.

Saturation with Respect to Ice

If the atmosphere over a particle of ice contains the same concentration of water vapor as that given off by the ice it is said to be **Saturated with Respect to Ice**. If the vapor concentration in the air is higher than the vapor pressure over the ice it is said to be **Supersaturated with Respect to Ice**. Some molecules condense onto the ice surface (Fig. 3.3).

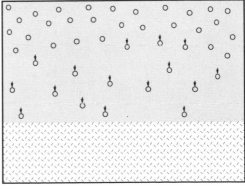

Fig. 3.3

Snow in the Air

Snowfall

Snowfall occurs when moist air, rising to a level where it is cooled below freezing, forms ice crystals which eventually fall to the ground as snow. The intensity, or rate of snowfall (measured in cm/hour), depends on how much moisture is available in the atmosphere and how fast the moist air rises. Many serious avalanche cycles are associated with higher than usual rates of snowfall.

Formation of Snow

In order for ice crystals to form, foreign particles are needed around which super-cooled water droplets can crystallize. These are called Freezing Nuclei and are generally composed of clay particles which are much scarcer than Condensation Nuclei and only become active at lower temperatures. The colder the temperature the more Freezing Nuclei become active to the point where at -40°C, supercooled water droplets freeze instantly. Once the initial crystallizing into ice has taken place it is possible that splinters of ice, breaking off from other crystals, may also act as freezing nuclei.

Eventually, a state is achieved where the cloud is composed of both ice crystals and supercooled water droplets. The difference in vapor pressure between ice and super-cooled water allows the ice crystals to grow at the expense of the supercooled droplets because the cloud, which is only saturated with respect to water, is supersaturated with respect to ice. Molecules of water vapor are constantly migrating from higher pressure regions over the water droplets to the lower pressure ice surface. The transformation into snow crystals gives travelling molecules the opportunity of finally achieving an orderly existence. The crystals continue to grow until they are heavy enough to escape from updrafts in the cloud formation and begin their journey groundward.

Snow Crystals

If you look closely at falling snow you'll notice that it's usually composed of bright crystalline particles of ice, either alone or matted together to form larger snowflakes. These snow crystals are six sided and vary from very thin hexagonal stars and plates to long columns or needles. Although the chance of two snow crystals being alike is remote they do form a number of fairly consistent types as shown in Fig 3.12. The basic form of a snow crystal is determined by the temperature at which it forms. Its size and any subsequent change depends on the amount of moisture available. To a lesser extent the degree of supersaturation modifies the crystal form and controls the rate of growth. Most crystal types form within a very small temperature range. For instance, the beautiful classic stellar crystals only grow between approximately -12°C and -16°C.

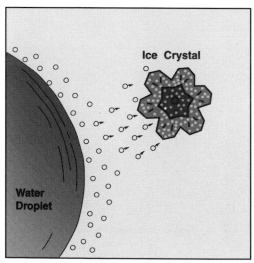

Fig. 3.4 Ice crystals grow at the expense of supercooled water droplets.

Crystal Types	
Type of Crystal	Temp. Range at formation
Thin hexagonal plates	0 to -3
Needles	-3 to -5
Hollow prismatic columns	-5 to -8
Hexagonal plates	-8 to -12
Stellars & dendrites	-12 to -16
Hexagonal plates	-16 to -25
Hollow prisms	-25 to -50

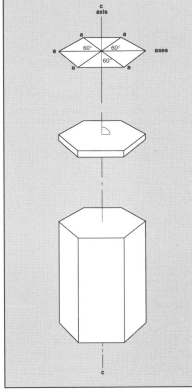

Fig. 3.5 The crystal form of ice. Crystals may grow either along the a-axis to form plates and dendritic crystals or along the c-axis to produce columns and needles.

Fig. 3.6 Above right. Plate crystal about 1 mm in diameter. Photo by Y. Furukawa, The Institute of Low Temperature Science, Sapporo.

Fig. 3.7 Right. Dendritic Crystal about 2.5 mm in diameter. Photo by Y Furukawa, The Institute of Low Temperature Science , Sapporo.

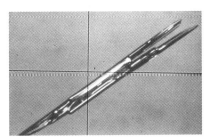

Fig. 3.8 Needle crystal approximately 3 mm long. Photo by Y. Furukawa, The Institute of Low Temperature Science, Sapporo.

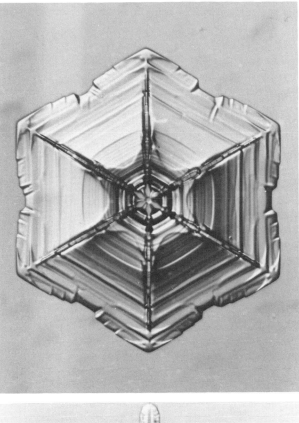

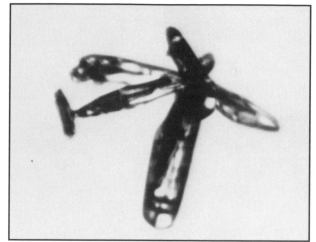

Fig. 3.9 A cluster of bullet-shaped crystals. Photo by Ron Perla

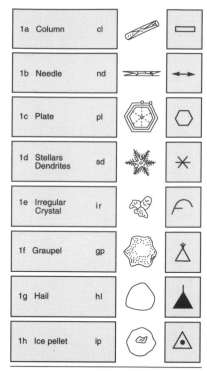

1a	Column	cl		
1b	Needle	nd		
1c	Plate	pl		
1d	Stellars Dendrites	sd		
1e	Irregular Crystal	ir		
1f	Graupel	gp		
1g	Hail	hl		
1h	Ice pellet	ip		

Fig. 3.12 International classification for precipitation particles. International Association of Scientific Hydrology.

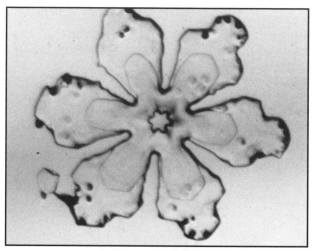

Fig. 3.10 Segmented crystal about 1 mm diameter. Photo by Ron Perla.

Falling Snow Crystals

The changes which take place in the form of snow crystals after their initial formation and before they reach the ground are important in evaluating avalanche hazard.

There are many factors which affect the crystal on its way to the ground: atmospheric conditions such as wind, turbulence, the temperature and moisture level in various layers of the clouds, coupled with the original form of the crystal and the total depth of the cloud, can cause the crystal to either grow or evaporate away, to melt into rain, or to break up into fragments from physical collisions.

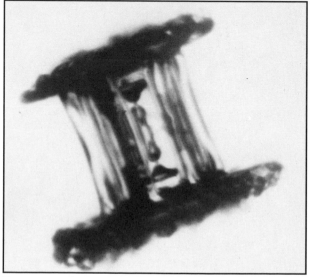

Fig. 3.11 Capped column. Photo by Ron Perla

56

Of particular interest is the way crystals grow after their initial formation. There are three basic ways.

Snowflakes are formed when individual crystals collide with other crystals in warm moist conditions to form conglomerates. The largest snowflakes are often composed of stellar crystals, although other crystal types can matt together in the same way.

Riming The second way in which crystals grow has a significant effect on new snow stability and on the development of hazard. This is riming, or growth by collision with supercooled water droplets which instantly freeze on contact with the crystal. While most snowfalls have crystals with some degree of rime, the more turbulent the air in the upper atmosphere, the more rime a crystal collects, and in some cases, with thick clouds and strong updrafts, the original crystal form becomes totally unrecognizable. In these stormy conditions the snow formed is known as **Graupel** or **Pellet Snow**. Graupel is often associated with the passage of a cold front. Dry **Granular Snow**, occasionally encountered at high altitudes or in very cold conditions is usually composed of clusters of moderately rimed crystals such as plates, bullets and columns. It has a dry powdery appearance and is prone to forming cohesive slabs even when there is very little wind.

Crystal growth The third form of growth is the continued growth of the original crystal to give larger and more intricate crystals.

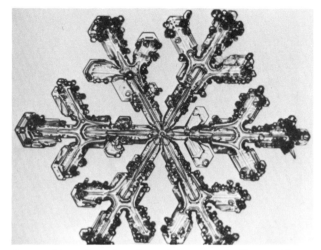

Fig. 3.13 Rimmed star-shaped crystal about 2 mm in diameter. Photo by Y. Furukawa, The Institute of Low Temperature Science. Sapporo.

Fig. 3.14 Heavily rimed star-shaped crystal. Photo by Ron Perla.

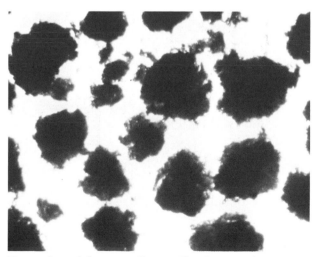

Fig. 3.15 Graupel about 2 mm diameter. Photo by Ron Perla.

Fig. 3.16 Rime-plastered rocks and vegetation. Photo by Chris Stethem.

Other forms of Snow or Ice

Different types of crystals, similar to snow crystals, form close to the surface of the earth under certain conditions of temperature and humidity. They are called **Non-Precipitated** forms of snow and ice. Two forms you should know about are **Rime** and **Hoarfrost**.

Rime is formed when droplets of supercooled water impinge on any object in their path. It has a dull white, non-crystalline appearance and is found deposited on the windward side of rocks, vegetation and sometimes whole mountainsides. Rime is a good indicator of wind direction. A ski pole standing outside overnight will often be found next morning with a feathery deposit of rime growing into the wind. The amount of fresh buildup can be related to wind speed; the longer the feathers or the thicker the buildup, the higher the wind speed.

Fig. 3.17 Feathers of rime growing into the wind are good indicators of past wind direction.

58

Hoarfrost is a bright, sparkling crystalline growth of crystals which can be found on, above or in some cases below the snow surface. It is formed in much the same way as snow crystals and could be considered the snow equivalent of dew. What happens is that daytime radiation allows the air above the snow surface to hold a substantial amount of water vapor. On a cold clear night when the snow surface is cooled by loss of heat to the atmosphere, the air becomes supersaturated with respect to the ice and water vapor condenses on the snowpack to forms a delightfully crisp, crystalline surface on which to ski known as Surface Hoar. In cold northern latitudes surface hoar will remain unchanged during clear sunny days in midwinter. A thick layer of 1 cm or more can persist in the snow cover for a considerable period of time after its formation. This weak layer acts as a potentially dangerous sliding surface for the snow above.

Fig. 3.18 The buried layer of surface hoar can be clearly seen about half-way down. Photo by Bruce Jamieson.

Fig. 3.19 Large surface hoar crystals approximately 4 cm long. Photo by Leon Kubbernus.

Another variety, **Crevasse Hoar**, can be found in spaces around rocks and trees, inside crevasses and in ice caves where over a period of several weeks, large crystals may form. The crystal illustrated in the photographs below is approximately 7.5 cm long and 5 cm across the open cup.

Hoarfrost is responsible for the fern-like patterns on windows and the delicate, glittering tracery on vegetation.

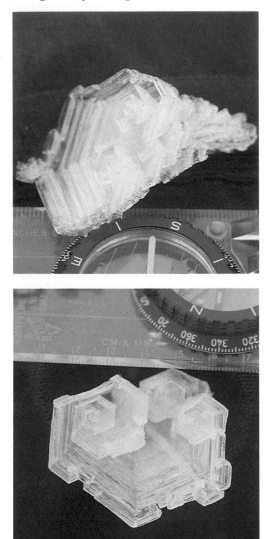

Fig. 3.20 Very large crevasse hoar crystals found in an ice cave at the snout of the Saskatchewan Glacier, Canadian Rockies.

Snow Crystals and Avalanche Hazard

Crystal Type Because of differences in shape and density some types of snow crystals have a greater tendency to create hazardous avalanche conditions than others.

Delicate stellar crystals and clusters of bullet-shaped crystals with little or no riming have some initial cohesion due to interlocking of the crystal branches. Because it usually has a density of less than $70 \, kg/m^3$, this form of snow sluffs off steeper slopes within a few days and doesn't form dangerous soft slabs. However, if the crystals are broken into fragments by strong or moderate winds they will pack together and form stiff wind-drifted slabs which are potentially very dangerous.

Needle and plate crystals falling in windless conditions produce almost immediate hazard from loose-snow avalanches. If followed by a snowfall of crystals with greater cohesion they will form a weak sliding layer within the snowpack.

Effect of Rime Rime builds up on snow crystals as they fall through the atmosphere. It not only increases the density but also gives more contact points allowing adjacent crystals to more readily bind together. See 'sintering' on page 68. In other words, the likelihood of slabs forming increases with the degree of riming.

Although partially rimed crystals allow greater initial stability, the condition can lead to a buildup of thick layers of snow before a slab releases. High intensity snowfalls of heavily rimed crystals deposited in strong winds forms tough, hard and unpredictable slabs. Rimed needles, in particular will form dense compact snow slabs up to $300 \, kg/m^3$.

Because of its high density (up to $250 \, kg/m^3$) and relatively low tensile strength, graupel readily forms slab when deposited in thick layers of 15 cm or more.

Snow on the Ground

Snow on the ground consists of many layers of solid precipitation modified by wind, sun or rain. These layers can be distinctly separate or can merge imperceptibly with one another. Weak layers, or lack of bond between layers, form sliding surfaces within the snowpack. The thickness of identifiable layers may vary from many centimeters of new snowfall to a millimeter or less of recrystallized snow. Because of continuous changes in temperature and pressure within the snowpack caused by varying meteorological conditions, the physical composition of

the snow is constantly changing until it either melts, evaporates or, in areas of permanent snow, consolidates to become glacier ice.

Use a magnifying glass to examine a sample of old, consolidated snow from 20 to 30 cm below the surface. If temperatures have been moderate you will see little trace of the original crystals. Instead there will be a mass of rounded ice particles called **Ice Grains** and a lot of vacant spaces called **Pore spaces**. The grains may be connected to each other by **Necks** of ice; the thicker the necks the stronger the snow structure.

Most avalanches slide at a weak layer in the snowpack or on a hard, smooth layer. An understanding of the layered composition of the snowpack is essential for evaluating avalanche hazard.

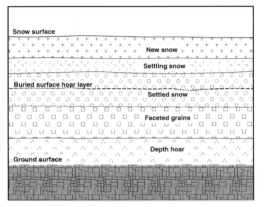

Fig. 3.21 Snow on the ground builds up in many layers.

Fig. 3.22 The snowpack consist of ice grains, often joined by necks of ice, and pockets of air called pore spaces. The black spheres are air bubbles in the solution used to hold the snow for photography. Photo by E. Akitaya, The Institute of Low Temperature, Science, Sapporo.

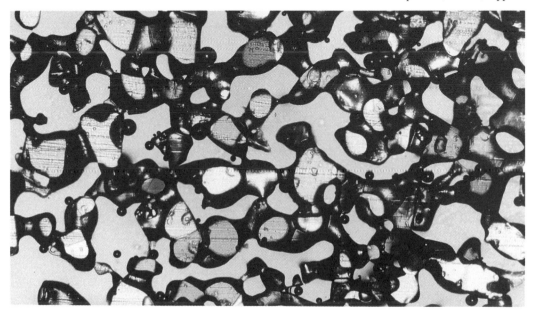

The Ground Surface

The temperature of the ground in temperate climates remains close to 0°C. This is due in part to the residual heat in the earth's surface but is mainly due to the insulating properties of fresh snow. Even in colder climates, where the ground is several degrees below freezing, there can be considerable temperature difference between the snow surface and the ground surface in cold weather. This difference in temperature has considerable significance in cold climates when the snowpack is shallow.

Temperature Gradient

The temperature gradient is the difference in temperature between two snow layers or between a snow layer and the ground expressed in terms of degrees Celsius per metre of depth. For example, consider one metre of snow lying on a ground surface whose temperature is 0°C. If the air temperature drops to -20°C there is a difference of 20°C in 1 metre of snow depth or 20°C/m.

Because the temperature gradient influences the movement of water molecules within the snowpack, it has a significant effect on changes in snow structure within the snowpack.

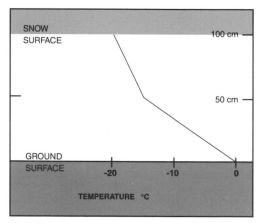

Fig. 3.23 The temperature gradient often varies throughout the snowpack. In this simplified diagram the upper portion has a temperature gradient of 10°C/m while the lower section is 30°C/m.

The Snow Surface and How it Changes

The snow surface is constantly changing. If temperatures remain below freezing and the surface is deprived of sun, conditions can remain constant for many days. Unfortunately there are several changes in weather conditions which will turn the ideal snowpack into something less than desirable.

Fresh, new snowfall leaves a bright, highly reflective surface which bounces most of the sun's heat back into the atmosphere. As the snow crystals break down, the surface becomes duller and the snowpack absorbs more of the sun's heat. Dust particles settle from the atmosphere further dulling the snow. Later in the season depressions appear in the surface called **Sun Cups**. Wind will form ripples much like sand on a beach; stronger winds will scour and re-deposit snow or form areas of dull, chalky-white, hard packed slab.

Simple observation of the snow surface can tell you a lot about past, present or potential avalanche hazard.

Surface roughness

The shape and depth of irregularities in the snow surface caused by wind, rain, uneven evaporation or uneven melting is a useful indicator of past weather conditions. For example, convex furrows running downhill in the snow surface is an indication of rain, with the depth of the channels giving a rough indication of the amount and duration of the rainfall.

Surface Penetration

Noting the amount of surface penetration by a person either on foot or on skis is a good indication of how much new snow has fallen and how fast it is settling. If you are breaking trail in fresh snow to mid calf depth (about 30 cm) you should be concerned about the stability of the new snow on steep slopes.

Effect of wind

One of the major forces altering the character of new snow is wind. Wind alters the snow layers you ski in by breaking up the crystals as they seek a place to settle, by battering them across the snow surface (saltation) and by redistributing them once they have settled. In addition, wind allows rapid evaporation from the snowpack by transporting water vapor away from the surface of the crystals.

The major effect of wind on the snow cover is the rapid loading of lee slopes with wind-blown snow. Large amounts of snow, deposited by strong winds, results in a rapid change in the equilibrium balance between the additional load of newly deposited snow and the strength of the bond between critical snow layers. The snowpack can only adjust to an increase in stress at a certain rate. If that rate is exceeded, then failure will occur. In practice, a steep slope loaded by wind-blown snow may release several times during a storm.

Windcrust, formed by the action of wind blowing across the surface of snow, is a hardened, crusted layer which forms a discontinuity in the snow on which further snowfalls can slide. When neither deep enough nor hard enough to support a persons weight it creates extremely tiresome travelling conditions.

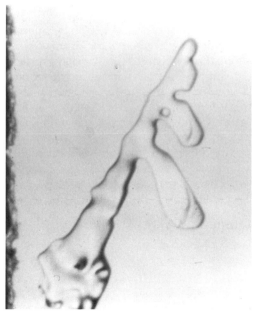

Fig. 3.25 Wind-broken crystal fragment. Photo by Ron Perla.

Fig. 3.26 Wind etching of the snow surface.

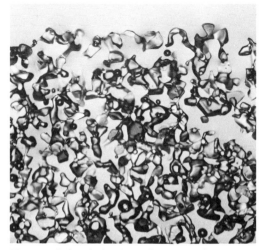

Fig. 3.24 wind-packed grains at the snow surface. Density 380 kg/m³, scale 15:1. Photo by E. Akitaya, The Institute of Low Temperature Science, Sapporo.

Effect of sun

On a sunny day after new snowfall, the snow will begin to develop a crust called **Sun Crust**. A minute amount of melting in the first few millimetres below the surface forms a slightly icy cohesive layer which gradually spreads down through the surface layers changing what was perfect skiing conditions one day into tricky, crusty conditions the next.

A few days of hot still weather in spring will result in a pitted snow surface. This type of crust, known as **Perforated Crust**, is formed by differential melting by the sun's rays. The portion of the ice grains which receive the greatest amount of radiation melt first leaving minute hollows in the snow which are enlarged as time progresses. The shape of the hollows depends upon the direction of the sun's rays and the angle at which the sun strikes the snow surface; wind and sun can combine to create many beautiful patterns. If the snow beneath is firm and the hollows not too big, perforated crust provides an excellent skiing surface.

Sun crust should not be confused with the sleek shiny ice glaze found on some slopes after a period of cold clear weather in spring and early summer.

Rain forms an icy crust on the surface which may develop into an icy impervious layer when covered by further snowfall. A November rainfall across Western Canada in 1979 was responsible for a rash of avalanche accidents ranging all the way from Whistler Ski area near Vancouver to Banff in the Canadian Rockies.

Ice Glaze is caused by deposition of rime on windward slopes. It often occurs within a specific altitude range and provides an excellent sliding layer when buried by fresh snowfall.

Fig. 3.28 Sun cups provide ready-made steps for these climbers on Mount Sir Sandford, British Columbia.

Do not forget that, given favorable conditions, layers of rain, sun, or wind crust can persist in the snowpack for many weeks and initiate several avalanche cycles before finally disappearing.

Fig. 3.27 Sun and wind combined to form this perforated crust near Mount Assiniboine, Canadian Rockies. Photo by Bob Sandford, courtesy Alberta Mountain Council.

Deposited Snow

In windless conditions snow falls uniformly over the mountains and, depending on temperature, can range from fluffy downlike stellar snow crystals to large, wet, heavy snowflakes. The initial properties of a snow layer depend on the crystal type, the amount of modification to the crystals and the meteorological conditions of wind and temperature near the surface of the ground at the time of deposition.

Snow accompanied by wind gives a different form of snowpack buildup. Snow tends to be deposited on the lee side of ridges or in gullies where the wind velocity drops. Over large areas the snow forms cohesive slabs of varying degrees of hardness, while smaller isolated slabs develop wherever there are minor changes in slope angle or orientation of terrain.

Snow can also be deposited by wind alone, blown from the windward side of a ridge to the lee side. The amount of snow and the speed of build-up should not be underestimated.

An unusually high rate of new snowfall, or a rapid deposition of old snow by wind, will cause a rapid increase in stress within the snowpack. Consequently there is a greater chance of weak layers within the snowpack failing.

Effect of Temperature

Snow is an unusual and unpredictable material. It possesses the same properties as most common engineering materials, but because it exists close to its melting point and responds rapidly to small changes in temperature these properties are difficult to measure. The temperature range at which we usually encounter snow is very small; from -20°C to just above 0°C. Above freezing, snow becomes wet and soggy, eventually melting; below -20°C there is little observable change from day to day.

Because the strength of a snow layer tends to decrease as the temperature rises towards freezing point it follows that a sudden rise in temperature will usually result in a decrease in stability. In practice, any sudden rise of 4° or 5°C is one of the major avalanche warning signs.

Density of Snow

The density of snow (the proportion of snow to air spaces) varies tremendously from light fluffy snow deposited under moderately cold, calm conditions to hard old wind-deposited slabs and eventually, if it does not melt first, to green glacier ice.

Snow layers on the ground contain a considerable amount of air. The density of a layer is measured by weighing a known volume of snow and the results expressed in one of two forms: either as a weight of snow per cubic metre (kilograms per cubic metre) or by specific gravity which has no dimensions. Specific gravity is a ratio between the weight of snow and the weight of an equal volume of water. In the case of snow it will always be less than one.

Typical Densities of Snow Layers

Type of snow	Density Kg/m3	Specific Gravity
Wild Snow	3	.003
Light new snow	30	.03
New snow - no wind	100	.10
Wind deposited snow	250	.25
Cornice snow	400	.40
Firn snow	600	.60
Glacier ice	800	.80

Adapted from table by M. de Quervain

Liquid Water Content

The amount of water in the snowpack is of considerable interest to the backcountry skier as any snow with a discernible liquid water content may have a significant effect on stability, either from the additional loading of the wet snow disturbing the equilibrium balance or from weak, cohesionless grains, formed below the wet layer by water seeping from above, creating a sliding layer.

Liquid water content may be estimated by trying to form a snowball. Moist snow (less than 3% water) will form a good snowball. Wet snow (3-8% water) will form a hard, solid snowball, but you will be unable to squeeze water from it. If you can squeeze water out the snow is termed "very wet' and contains 8-15% free water.

Strength of Snow

The strength of a snow layer is its ability to resist stresses exerted on it. Strength varies according to the type of stress applied (compressive, tensile or shear), the rate at which the stress is applied, the amount of deformation (strain) and the rate at which the snow deforms.

Because snow is not a homogeneous material its strength is dependent upon the density of the layer, the type and size of snow particles in the layer, and the temperature. Generally the strength of a layer increases with density; a layer of old firn snow may be 1000 times stronger than one of recently settled snow.

The table opposite gives typical strengths of various types of snow and how the strength of the snow may change over time.

Hardness

Hardness is the resistance to penetration of an object into snow. When we poke our fist or fingers into the wall of a snowpit, we are measuring hardness. The measurement of hardness is subjective and depends upon what instruments we are pressing into the snow. There is a direct relationship between hardness and strength. Refer to the section on snowpits (page 111) for the hardness terms used in snow science and how they relate to the hand tests we use in snowpits.

Grain Shape and Size

The shape and size of ice grains found within the snowpack have a direct bearing on snow stability. Grain shape has been classified into a number of distinct types such as rounded, faceted, cup shaped. In the next section on how the snow changes over time we will be discussing the significance of the various grain shapes and how these shapes change from one type to another due to changes in temperature and temperature gradients within the snowpack. As the shapes change so does the size of the grains. See page 112 for tables of grain shapes and sizes.

Strength of Various Types of Snow		
Snow Type	Strength	Variation with Time
Recently deposited snow.	Low to very low.	Decreases with time, although some forms of snow crystals will have initial strength because of interlocking of crystal branches.
Broken wind-packed particles.	Medium to high.	Rapid strength increase due to close packing and rapid sintering.
Settled snow with rounded grains.	High to very high.	Increases with time and density. Offset by a decrease in strength with increasing grain size.
Settled snow with a high proportion of faceted grains.	Medium.	Decreases with increasing growth rate and grain size.
Depth Hoar.	Low to very low.	Decreases with increasing growth rate and crystal size. Increases with increasing density.
Surface Hoar.	Extremely low.	May exist in fragile state for long periods when buried in cold snow.
Melt-freeze snow.	High when frozen.	Strength increases with number of melt-freeze cycles. As liquid content increases, snow turns to slush with little strength.

Fig. 3.29 Snow overhanging a signpost shows the tensile strength of a cohesive mass of settled snow. Photo by Rick Kunelius, courtesy Canadian Parks Service.

Creep & Glide

Snow can at the same time be both brittle and viscous. If you place your foot in cold snow it will fail by fracturing under the sudden load. On the other hand snow lying on a steep roof will flow (creep) under gravity like a liquid, deforming under its own weight to hang over the edge. Cracks may form higher up on the roof as the snow fails in tension. The whole layer may move slowly and steadily (glide) down the roof or one layer may slide off on another — a shear failure between layers.

If snowpack is lightly and slowly loaded it will deform gradually and settle due to the rearrangement of water molecules among the ice grains. Conversely, if the snowpack is loaded rapidly, by a heavy snowfall or by strong wind deposition, the stresses in the snowpack do not have time to adjust viscously and brittle fracture takes place.

Fig. 3.30 If you step down into snow, it will fail in compression due to brittle fracture of the connections between ice grains.

Fig. 3.31 Snow sliding down a roof demonstrates both tensile and shear failure. Creep and glide tend to increase the tensile forces within an inclined snowpack.

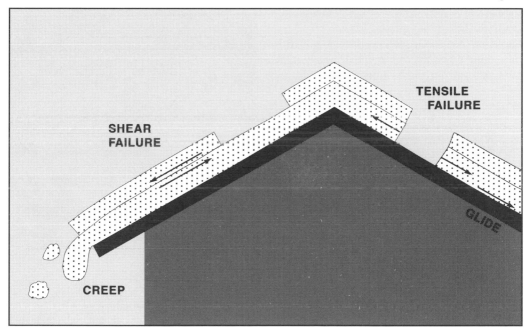

Settlement and Strengthening

Skiers automatically recognize a number of different types of snow conditions and classify them according to the ease or difficulty of travel. Snow conditions, particularly changes in snow conditions, may be related to the development of avalanche hazard.

Think of a fresh fall of cold **New Snow** in relatively windless conditions. (The term 'New Snow' refers to snow immediately after it has fallen and before it has materially changed from its initial snow crystal condition). Soon after it has fallen, depending on the temperature, it will begin to settle. Thirty centimetres of new snow, initially containing 85 - 90% of air, may settle to 20 cm; so that instead of sinking knee deep, the skier will only leave tracks a few centimetres deep. What causes these changes and what is their significance for the recreational skier?

Metamorphism

Metamorphism means "change of form" and is the name given to changes in the structure of snow within the snowpack, and also to changes in the snowpack itself due to the temperature of the snow and the difference in temperature between the various layers.

A small temperature gradient (see page 60) will result in the rounding of ice grains, and growth of the larger grains at the expense of the smaller ones. A large temperature gradient will result in a recrystallization process resulting in faceted crystals, and in extreme cases hollow, cup-shaped crystals of depth hoar. These processes have in the past been known as Destructive and Constructive metamorphism, Equi-Temperature & Temperature Gradient metamorphism and are now referred to by the scientific community as **"Equilibrium forms or Kinetic Growth forms"**.

We will refer to the form of the snow particles as **rounded or faceted**, and to the processes involved as **rounding and recrystallization**.

The Process of Rounding

When outside temperatures are moderate or when the snowpack is deep, the temperature gradients within the snowpack will be small. Snow will then change by a process known as "rounding". The natural process of minimizing surface area breaks down the intricate crystalline snow structure of the ice crystals into smaller, more rounded ice grains. At the same time, because of the reduction in volume of the snow particles, the snowpack consolidates and settles. When snow is first

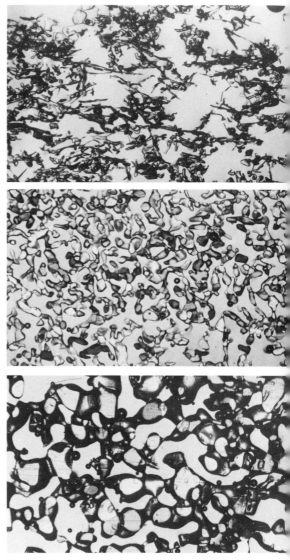

Fig. 3.32 Three stages in the process of rounding. From top to bottom: new snow with a density of 100 kg/m³, rounded ice grains showing no evidence of original crystalline form, well sintered grain with a density of 460 kg/m³. Scale 15:1. Photo by E. Akitaya, The Institute of Low Temperature Science, Sapporo.

deposited it is light and fluffy, the crystal branches interlocking to form a cohesive mass. The snow during this period is stable and will remain plastered on steep slopes and rock bands. After a period of time, water molecules are transferred by vapor movement from the extremities to the body of the crystal, the destruction of the interlocking branches result in a critical period during which the snow becomes unstable. Eventually, the ice grains lose all sign of their previous crystalline structure and become more and more rounded. The larger ice grains grow at the expense of the smaller particles resulting in a uniformity of size within each snow layer.

At temperatures close to freezing (0°C to -5°C) change is rapid, the snow layers consolidating and becoming denser, stronger and more stable in a relatively short period of time. As temperatures drop, the process slows down, until at -40°C it is almost non-existent.

In order to avoid periods of instability, you should try to estimate how fast the process of rounding is progressing. The time before the snow becomes stable can vary from a day or two to several weeks depending on temperature. Small sluffs from steep ground, or snow falling off trees are visual indications that rounding is taking place. In early writings on avalanche hazard in the Alps, Arnold Lunn states that, *"A good rule is to mistrust all steep slopes after a fresh fall until the pine trees are free from snow"*. Unfortunately, vagaries of climate and weather create exceptions to such rules of thumb.

Fig. 3.34 When the snow falls from trees you know that settlement and strengthening of the snowpack is taking place.

Powder snow is snow which has undergone the first stages of rounding. It has lost its initial fluffy crystalline character and is beginning to settle, becoming duller and less cohesive.

Metamorphism, speeded up by the weight of additional layers of new snowfall produces **Settled** snow. This is the light cohesive snow beloved by the telemark skier or snowboarder; it's easy to turn in, yet firm enough to easily initiate turns.

It's interesting to note that strengthening due to the additional weight of further snowfalls doesn't take place as rapidly on slopes of 30° as it does on level ground. This is because the vertical force varies with slope angle, and snow on steeper slopes is often not as well consolidated. This is one reason why you must examine small slopes of the same steepness when evaluating a suspect avalanche slope.

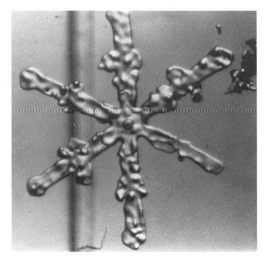

Fig. 3.33 Stellar Crystals showing initial rounding due to rounding and some riming. Photo by Chris Stethem.

How Snow Gains Strength

You've probably noticed that a trail broken in soft new snow the previous day will harden overnight. This packing and hardening process, where the snow gains strength by the joining together of ice grains, is called **Sintering**.

In the case of the ski trail, the snow crystals or ice grains are forced together by the weight of the skier. However, over a period of time the natural settlement of the snowpack (see page 68) and the weight of additional layers will also result in the ice grains being pressed together. This pressure creates stresses at the boundary where the grains press together resulting in the migration of water molecules in the area of the grain bond to form boundaries (necks) between grains. At temperatures just below freezing, the grain boundary grows, forming stronger bonds between ice grains. On rewarming, the necks between ice grains will be reduced, weakening or destroying the bond between grains.

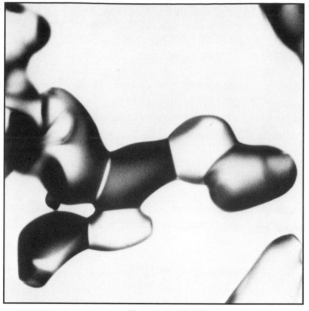

Fig. 3.35 Ice grains with necks. Photo by Ron Perla.

In the absence of appreciable wind or extremes of temperature the process of settlement and strengthening makes an ideal snowpack, with light unconsolidated snow near the surface gradually getting denser, more firmly packed, as the depth increases.

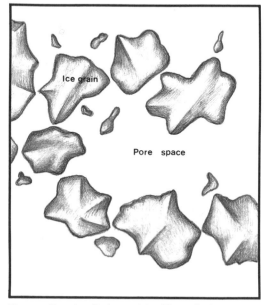
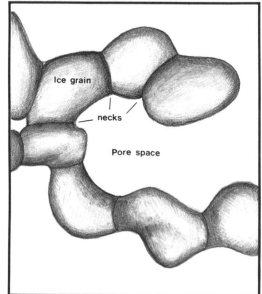

Fig. 3.36 Sintering. Grains are joined by necks forming between ice grains forced into contact with each other.

Changes due to Cold

Crystal Growth

Crystal growth is the result of a relatively large temperature difference between two layers within the snowpack. For instance, the loose, sugar-snow, found in shallow, early-season snowpacks in some snow climates is the result of large temperature differences between the ground surface and the snow surface. In other cases, layers of loose snow grains may be found in the upper layers of buried crusts formed by a high temperature gradient between the warmer crust and the colder snow above.

Growth occurs because of an upward movement of water molecules within the pore spaces in the snowpack, the rounded ice grains formed at more moderate temperatures begin to take on a more angular form as water molecules move from the top of a grain and are deposited on the bottom of the grain above. This process is called **Recrystallization**.

Fig. 3.37 Depth Hoar Crystal 4 mm long. Photo by Ron Perla.

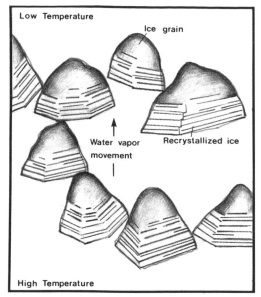

Fig. 3.38 Depth hoar forms when water vapor, due to a large temperature gradient, recrystallizes on the bottom of ice grains.

The Significance of Recrystallization

Recrystallization leads to a weakening of snow layers within the snowpack. Such layers can be microscopically thin — and difficult to detect — or consist of a metre or more of large cup-shaped crystals with very little strength and which become cohesionless when disturbed.

Recrystallization due to large temperature gradients is prevalent in colder climates early in the winter when the snowpack is both shallow and unconsolidated. Extreme growth occurs when temperatures are very cold — below -20°C.

In denser snow, where smaller pore spaces allow little space for the growth of individual crystals, large temperature gradients result in faceted grains. In very dense snow, with small pore spaces faceting may not occur.

While we normally think of recrystallization occurring vertically within the snowpack, large temperature differences between objects such as rocks buried in the snow and the surrounding snow can result in recrystallization horizontally from the object leading to localized weakening. See the discussion on "Weak Spots" on page 147.

71

Grain shape classification recognizes several stages of the recrystallization process. The two main ones are faceted grains and cup-shaped crystals (depth hoar). For practical purposes we will discuss the two separately, but remember that it is the same process at a different stage and taking place under different conditions of temperature gradient and snow density

Faceted Grains

The formation of faceted grains marks the beginning of crystal growth which is characterized by the development of angular grains with flat crystal faces or facets, just like the faces on a cut diamond. As long as there is sufficient temperature difference between individual grains in the snowpack, crystal growth due to the temperature gradient will successfully compete with the tendency for rounding. If the size of the initial ice grains is large enough and the pore spaces big enough, the process of crystal growth will continue and large cup crystals with well-developed stepped surfaces will form. These large crystals are called depth hoar.

Faceted grains can develop at the base of the snowpack, in layers within the snowpack and even in the surface layers of the snowpack. It is the layers buried within the snowpack which are of most concern to the backcountry traveller as, in many instances, they are very hard to detect.

Typical Faceted Layers

At the base of the snowpack. In cold weather some faceting occurs in the lower layers of almost all shallow snowpacks. How much the process will weaken the snowpack depends upon the temperature, the temperature gradient and the density of the snow. As temperature gradients moderate as a result of further snowfall or warmer temperatures, the process of rounding will prevail and the snowpack will be strengthened due to sintering. However, if cold conditions continue, and the snow is not too dense, depth hoar will form, substantially weakening the base of the snowpack.

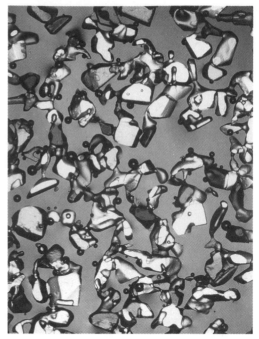

Fig. 3.39 Faceted grains. Photo by E. Akitaya. The Institute of Low Temperature Science. Sapporo.

Radiation recrystallization. On clear dry days during the winter and early spring, slopes with a southerly exposure will absorb enough of the sun's heat for a thin freeze-thaw crust to form a centimetre or so below the surface even though the temperature of the snow surface may still be well below freezing due to infrared cooling. The difference in temperature between the cold surface snow and the warmer snow beneath allows recrystallization of the snow on top of the smooth freeze-thaw crust. These thin layers of recrystallized snow form weak, poorly bonded layers when buried beneath further snowfalls.

Areas which are susceptible to this phenomena are described as having a "Radiation snow climate". A good example is the San Juan Range of S.E. Colorado.

In order to achieve this form of recrystallization a delicate radiation balance is required; too much solar radiation or too little infrared cooling will lead either to Firnspiegel or to melting and suncrust formation. Unfortunately, radiation recrystallization is difficult for the tourer to detect and usually can only be surmised after careful examination and testing of the snowpack.

Surface layers of faceted crystals. At high altitudes and in polar regions, a significant layer of faceted crystals may form in the top layers of the snowpack after a protracted cold spell (-25°C to -30°C for a week or more). Described by early ski runners in the Alps as resembling "raw rice", these large loose faceted crystals are the result of recrystallization in snow grains which have undergone normal settling. Because the size attainable by faceting depends upon the initial size of the ice grains and the open space around them, these grains rarely exceed 3 mm in diameter.

When covered by subsequent snowfall they form weak layers in the snowpack which are often responsible for avalanches at higher elevations.

While forming an ideal surface layer for skiing down, climbing up through this type of snow on skis can be frustrating and usually requires a low angle of ascent to get any reasonable grip.

Fig. 3.40 Faceted Crystal approximately 1.5 mm diameter. Photo by Ron Perla.

Thin layers within the snowpack. Thin layers of recrystallized grains can form over a period of time within the snowpack as a result of strong temperature gradients between layer of significantly different density. Such layers have been found above crusts where the temperature of the crust is higher than the temperature of the snow above, and eventually result in a mechanical weakening of the upper layers of the crust region. These layers are very difficult for the backcountry traveller to detect.

Depth Hoar

When there's a large temperature difference between grains and relatively large spaces between grains, a more advanced type of crystal growth takes place. This process forms delicate, hexagonal cup-shaped crystals known as Depth Hoar or Sugar Snow. As new, individual cohesionless crystals are created, the former bond between the ice grains is destroyed, thus weakening the bottom layers of the snowpack considerably. Most extreme early in the season, depth hoar not only makes an unstable base for future snowfalls, but also makes for extremely tiresome skiing conditions in which the tourer breaks through into bottomless sugar snow with each step.

Fig. 3.41 Depth Hoar Crystals with a density of 290 kg/m³, scale 15:1. Photo by E. Akitaya, The Institute of Low Temperature Science, Sapporo.

If cold temperatures persist, the process of crystal growth works its way up through the snow cover with layers as much as one metre thick not unknown in the Canadian Rockies. The size of depth hoar crystals typically varies from 4 - 10 mm long, although larger crystals may form in extreme conditions. The largest crystals are found at the bottom of the snowpack and around the base of trees and rocks. As the crystals grow larger, the lateral bonds between grains disappear, resulting in a snowpack composed of large, cup-shaped striated hollow crystals arranged in columns — very fragile snow which has almost completely recrystallized.

The final stage in the growth of depth hoar at high temperature gradients in low density snow is the development of very large (10 - 20 mm) columnar crystals which have the c-axis (see Fig. 3.5 page 55) horizontal. Some bonding occurs as a result of packing due to the weight of snow layers above and there is some strengthening of the snow layer. Depth hoar crystals are a very durable crystal form and once formed will often be present at the bottom of the snowpack for the remainder of the season.

Fig. 3.42 Columnar depth hoar cup crystal approximately 10 mm long. Photo by Ron Perla.

During the early part of the season, if the snowpack remains shallow during extended cold spells, the snowpack may be composed entirely of faceted and depth hoar crystals. Trail breaking is very tiresome, and the whole snowpack will avalanche down to the ground, with the cohesionless crystals running freely around rocks or trees. A surprising number of skiers are caught in small depth hoar slides in December and January in the Canadian Rockies. Most of them are able to stand up, brush off the granular crystals, and carry on skiing. However some parties of ski mountaineers have taken some long, and usually fatal, rides over cliffs or into crevasses from very small depth hoar slides.

As the season progresses, the weight of additional snowfalls will result in a toughening of the depth hoar layer due to packing and sintering. The larger depth hoar crystals at the bottom of the snowpack do not necessarily form the weakest layer any longer; many avalanches are the result of failure at the interface between the depth hoar and faceted layers above.

Although the bottom layer of depth hoar gains some strength during the season, it take little change in weather conditions to destroy the fragile bonds. Old depth hoar becomes incredibly rotten if the snowpack warms up quickly due to percolating water or very warm weather in the spring, resulting in impossible skiing conditions. Descending from the high mountains with heavy packs one April, we fell waist deep, right through to the ground, every few metres for the last 2 km back to the highway.

Snowpack Metamorphism

Throughout the season in many climates the snowpack alternates between rounding and faceting with rounding predominating as spring approaches. In certain conditions both types of metamorphism may be present in the snowpack at the same time, although one will usually predominate. This can happen after a fresh fall of snow in cold weather; in the surface layers rounding will be busy breaking down the original intricate shape, while at the same time faceting will be taking place at the bottom of the snowpack. To complicate matters even further rounding can occur in recrystallized layers; for example the rounding of edges of large faceted crystals as they develop.

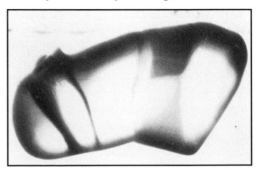

Fig. 3.43 Faceted Crystal showing evidence of rounding. Photo by Ron Perla.

Snow at Higher Temperatures

The Melt-Freeze Process

When the sun is sufficiently strong to melt the top layers of the snow-pack during the day, and when nighttime temperatures fall below 0°C, cycles of freezing and thawing will occur. In this process, called **Melt-freeze Metamorphism**, smaller grains will melt before larger ones and so during the course of a number of melt-freeze cycles larger grains will grow at the expense of smaller ones. The meltwater wetting the surface of these larger grains, eventually re-freezes and firmly cements the grains together. MF-grains have a tendency to freeze together in clusters, leaving large pore spaces within the snowpack.

During the melting cycle enough water may be produced to percolate through channels and pore spaces into the lower layers where they can form lubricating layers adjacent to the ground, impervious layers within the snowpack, or freeze into areas of ice called ice lenses.

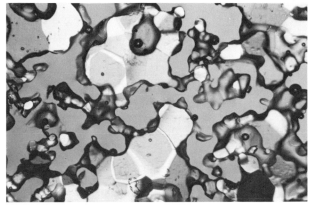

Fig. 3.44 Melt-freeze grains. Larger grains grow at the expense of smaller ones, grains group together and pore spaces are enlarged. Photo by E. Akitaya, The Institute of Low Temperature Science, Sapporo.

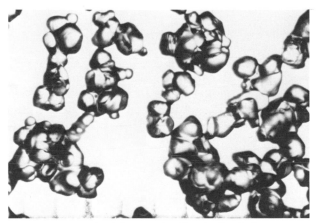

Fig. 3.45 Clusters of melt-freeze grains. Photo by Ron Perla.

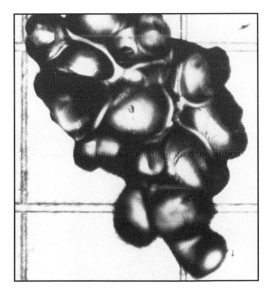

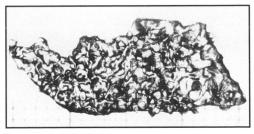

Fig. 3.46 A small section of ice crust approximately 20 mm long. Photo by Chris Stethem.

Fig. 3.47 A refrozen melt-freeze cluster shows the strength of a frozen layer. Photo by Ron Perla.

The major cause of melting of the snowpack is heat from the sun which is maximum at noon when the sun is highest. This implies that the most dangerous time for wet snow avalanches is between noon and early evening when freezing begins again. Of course, this rule does not apply if the overnight air temperature remains above freezing. This point is well illustrated by a report of an early morning wet slab avalanche, *"On Easter Sunday, at 8:30 the Glory Bowl on Teton Pass, Wyoming released. More than half of the large bowl fractured 3 feet deep and buried the highway below 25 feet deep and 240 feet in length. Two skiers had put tracks in the path earlier in the morning, and another group of five skiers were preparing to ski the bowl. The avalanche released while they were sipping tea at the edge of the bowl."*

Spring Snow Is the name commonly used for softened MF-grains. This form of snow varies from small early melt-freeze grains to large well-formed grains which, when wet, slide over each other with very little friction. The best skiing conditions occur shortly after melting begins and last until the snow finally saturated with meltwater becomes heavy and soggy. Spring snow takes several days to develop from new snow and during this interim period suncrust may make skiing impossible. Try moving to slopes of a different orientation; follow the sun around.

Rotten Snow Rotten snow is common in late spring in climates which favor the formation of appreciable amounts of depth hoar during the winter. When old depth hoar layers become saturated, they loose any mechanical strength which they may have once possessed. One result of this condition is the wet snow avalanching in spring which cleans off the snow cover right down to the ground. Travel, especially in late afternoon, can be exhausting, with the tourer sinking thigh deep in heavy wet snow which then collapses inwards on top of the skis burying them.

Meltwater Crust Meltwater crust is formed when snow melted during MF-metamorphism refreezes in the top layers only, leaving wet, unfrozen grains below. Such a crust may easily bear the weight of a skier in the early morning but later on when the day warms up, will weaken to create frustrating, leg-breaking conditions.

Firnspiegel Firnspiegel, or Firn Mirror, is the result of subsurface melting due to intense solar radiation during cold clear weather in spring or summer. The meltwater eventually forms a thin surface layer of clear ice — a highly reflective background for climbing or skiing photographs given the right slope angle and good lighting — which acts like a greenhouse allowing melting of the snow just beneath.

Firnspiegel is an excellent skiing surface, giving a firm bite to the ski as it is turned.

Fig. 3.48 The bright mirror-like surface of firnspiegel.

Older forms of Snow

So far I've described new snow in the season it has fallen. However, there is a limit to the amount of densification which can occur due to rounding alone, and once the ice grains have achieved a uniform, more or less spherical shape, two other processes are needed to cause a further increase in density. One of these, the melt-freeze process has already been covered. The other process, known as **Pressure Metamorphism**, is the primary mechanism in the formation of glacier ice. The separate grains are deformed and pressed together by the weight of additional snow layers until finally the pore spaces within the snowpack are so closed up they no longer allow the movement of water vapor through the snow.

Firn Snow Firn snow can be defined either as snow which has passed through several cycles of melting and freezing or as snow which has survived the spring thaw to become part of a permanent snowpatch or glacier. During the day it takes a lot of energy to break its dense structure down into loose grains which consequently freeze at night into a solid mass again.

Some Unusual Forms of Snow

Wild snow Wild snow is snow which has fallen in complete calm at very low temperatures. Resembling goose down, it's extremely light (it contains 97% to 99% air) and lies very loosely with the crystals hardly touching each other; you can walk or ski through it and feel no resistance. Wild snow I've seen in the Canadian Rockies appears to be made up of fine spatial dendrites, thin needles and a small proportion of whole stellar crystals. It's extremely unstable and will flow almost like a liquid down steep slopes. Although the avalanches it generates are usually harmless, large destructive avalanches have been reported in the Alps when great depths of wild snow gained additional density during the descent. Very often the frequent sluffing which occurs during and shortly after a fall of wild snow has a stabilizing effect on the fresh layer.

Diamond Dust Diamond dust is another form of ice crystal which occurs in very cold clear conditions. They're often seen early in the day as tiny glittering crystals floating in the atmosphere a few metres above the ground. It's believed that these minute crystals are formed during a temperature inversion when air a short distance above the ground is warmer than the air next to the ground.

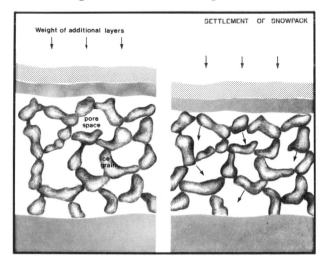

Fig. 3.49 The snowpack gains density and strength by a combination of rounding and the weight of additional layers of snowfall.

Fig. 4.1 Slab avalanches on all sides. Photo by André Roch.

4

Snow Avalanches

Avalanches fall when the weight of accumulated snow on a slope exceeds the forces within the snowpack or between the snowpack and the ground which holds the snow in place. The balance between these forces can be changed by further snowfall, by internal changes in the snow cover, or by the weight of a single skier. The often small force required to start the snow sliding is called an **avalanche trigger.**

There are two types of snow avalanches; loose-snow avalanches which originate in cohesionless snow and which start from one point, gathering more and more snow as they descend and slab avalanches which start when a large area of cohesive snow begins to slide at the same time.

Both types occur in wet and dry snow, either sliding down on a layer of snow within the snowpack or along the ground surface. Large avalanches can attain sufficient speed for some of the snow to become airborne.

Loose-snow Avalanches

Loose-snow avalanches start at one point on the snow cover and grow in size as they descend. They occur in snow with very little internal cohesion when the steepness of the slope exceeds the angle at which snow will cling to the snowpack. The critical angle, the angle formed by snow which is on the verge of sliding, is called the **angle of repose**.

Release is progressive and starts with a small, initially insignificant wedge of snow breaking away. Maybe the snow has collapsed internally because of surface melting or maybe it has been disturbed by some external force such as sluffs falling from the rocks above. There is no definite fracture line and the bed surface — the layer on which the snow slides — is not usually identifiable.

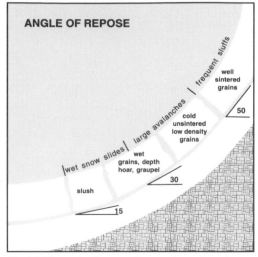

ANGLE OF REPOSE

frequent sluffs

well sintered grains

50

cold unsintered low density grains

large avalanches

wet snow slides

wet grains, depth hoar, graupel

30

slush

15

Fig. 4.2 The angle of repose of a snow layer depends upon grain size and shape, temperature and the wetness of the snow.

Fig. 4.3 Typical loose-snow avalanches in the Cariboo Mountains of British Columbia. Photo by Alf Skrastins.

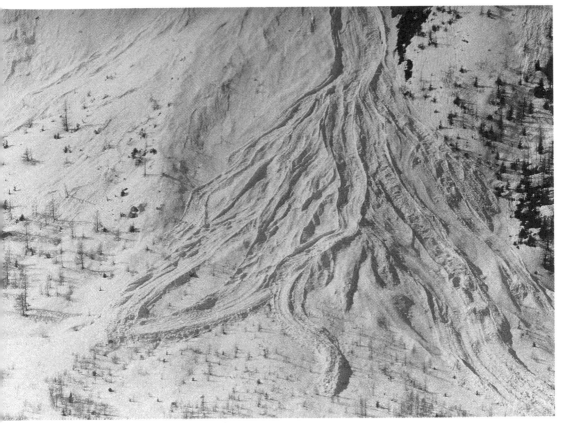

Fig. 4.4 Wet loose-snow slides down a gully in the Val Veni, Courmayer. Photo by André Roch.

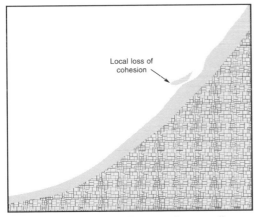

Local loss of cohesion

Fig. 4.5 Loose snow avalanches start when a small wedge of snow breaks away from the surface. From the Avalanche Handbook.

Occurrence Loose-snow avalanches can be observed at all times of the year in the mountains, but happen most frequently during the winter snow season. They often fall as numerous small sluffs during or shortly after a storm, removing snow from steep upper slopes and either stabilizing lower slopes or loading them with additional snow.

Wet loose-snow avalanches occur in spring and summer in all mountain ranges. Large avalanches of this type, lubricated and weighed down by meltwater or rain can travel long distance and have tremendous destructive power. Such avalanches are usually confined to coastal ranges which have relatively high temperatures and frequent rain.

Slope angle The slope angle required for loose snow to slide depends upon the temperature and the type of snow lying on the slope. Four conditions, either acting alone or in combination may lead to loose-snow avalanching.

— Very light fluffy snow deposited under windless conditions will initially cling to slopes of 50° to 55°, but because the snow lacks internal cohesion, it will eventually slide off as harmless sluffs before any great depth can accumulate.

— Cold, dry, granular snow and graupel will bounce and roll off steep slopes, falling as a constant stream onto easier-angled slopes below.

— Dry, or slightly damp powder snow deposited in light winds will develop enough cohesion to adhere to slopes of 40° to 50°. After a period of time, depending on temperature, changes in the structure of the snow will reduce internal cohesion and release small sluffs.

— Wet granular snow, lubricated by meltwater or rain has a very low internal friction and will slide on slopes as shallow as 15°.

In areas such as the Pacific Coast Ranges, the Andes and the Himalaya, snow from warm moist air plasters walls and faces as steep as 50° to 60°, where it stays in significant deposits.

Hazard Although relatively small, dry loose-snow avalanches can easily dislodge the skier or ski mountaineer from a safe stance and take him for a ride over cliff bands or into a crevasse. Most winter ice climbers are familiar with fresh snow cascading down the climb from above; in these conditions you should be particularly careful when negotiating steep snow slopes between pitches. Snow falling from steep upper slopes in this manner can either stabilize the lower slopes, load them with an additional weight of snow, or in extreme cases trigger dangerous slab avalanches.

Wet loose-snow avalanches — especially when triggered by rain — are extremely dangerous, often travelling long distances with tremendous destructive power. Wet loose-snow sluffs, although not dangerous in themselves, are a hazard the summer climber should be aware of.

Fig. 4.6 Sluffs of loose snow create problems for ice climbers. Raymond Jotterand on Bourgeau Left-hand, Canadian Rockies, Photo by Gregory Spohr.

Slab Avalanches

A slab avalanche occurs when a large area of cohesive snow begins to slide on a weak layer within the snowpack or on smooth ground. The consistency of the snow can vary from soft powder which loses all its cohesion on release to tough hard snow which deposits blocks measuring many cubic metres at the bottom of a slope. Slab avalanches are readily identified by the usually well-defined fracture line at the point where the moving mass of snow breaks away from the rest of the snowpack.

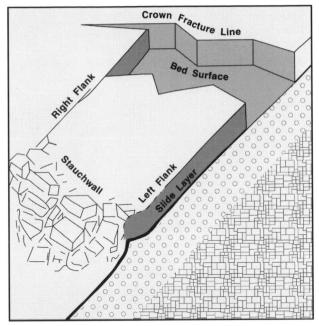

Fig. 4.7 Slab avalanche nomenclature.

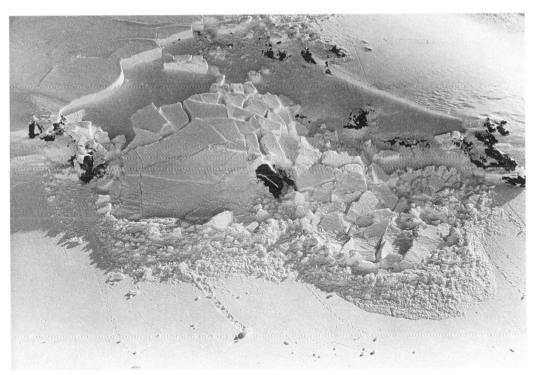

Fig. 4.8 A small wind slab avalanche on the Dorftali, Davos.
Photo by André Roch.

Release Because of the initial stressed condition, slab release is very rapid. Slabs fracture when the load of snow over a weak layer exceeds the strength of that layer. In some cases there may be initial settling of the snow at the moment of fracture.

Weak layers within the snowpack such as depth hoar, surface hoar, weak bond at rain or sun crust, temporary lack of riming or change of crystal type during a storm are all caused by many combinations of meteorological conditions. Often these weak layers are quite thin relative to the thickness of the slab, perhaps as little as 1:10 to 1:1000 and have densities not noticeably different from slab densities which vary from 90 to 450 Kg per cubic metre with an average of around 250 Kg per cubic metre. Soft slabs are easily released by skiers, though not necessarily by the first skier to cross the slope. As slabs become harder their behavior becomes more unpredictable; they may allow several people to ski across before releasing. It's believed they're susceptible to rapid temperature changes, both sudden warming and sudden cooling. It's been calculated that for normal density settled snow a drop in temperature of 10 C would cause a snow slope 300 m wide to contract 2 cm. Early ski mountaineers in the Alps noticed that avalanche sometimes occurred when shadows struck a previously sun-warmed slope.

Fig. 4.9 These two photographs of a skier-released avalanche are excellent examples of quick slab release. Note how the snow fractures, cracks and starts moving all at the same time. Read the discussion on "weak spots" on page 147 and take another look at these pictures. Photo by Rudolf Ludwig.

Occurrence The majority of soft-slab avalanches fall during or shortly after a storm when slopes are loaded with new snow at a critical rate. Usually, only the new snow layer releases. Fortunately for the traveller, **Direct-action** or Storm-induced slab avalanches are usually predictable; the old rule of never travelling in avalanche terrain for a few days after a storm still holds good.

At higher elevations, because of different harsher meteorological conditions, instability can persist for many days. Slabs release between storms without warning. These **Delayed-action** or Non storm-induced avalanches are the major hazard facing the skier in the dry cold ranges of the world during early winter or during low snowfall years simply because they are so difficult to predict. Such avalanches claimed eleven lives in seven separate incidents between December 1976 and April 1977 in the mountains of Western Canada.

Slope angle Slab avalanches release most frequently on slopes between 30° and 45°. On slopes of less than 25° snow tends to fracture and settle without sliding. Sometimes they occur on steeper slopes when there is a high rate of deposition in collection areas such as bowls and gullies.

Formation Soft slab forms over widespread areas during heavy storms, and is associated with moderate wind speeds, high humidity and, in some cases, rimed snow crystals. On the other hand, hard slab tends to form in localized areas such as the lee sides of ridges at higher elevations above timberline. It usually requires low temperatures and snow to be deposited by strong winds blowing for prolonged periods of time. Frequently, hard slabs are underlaid by a weak layer of depth hoar which fails to support the slab, and which accounts for the characteristic hollow feeling and the drop of a few centimetres when the slab fails. Snowfall isn't a necessary prerequisite; high winds picking up and redepositing snow to the lee side of ridges can also result in their formation. In high mountains slab occurs at all times of the year. How long it lasts depends upon the temperature.

Hazard Slab avalanches are the worst hazard the skier is likely to encounter. They are much more dangerous than dry loose-snow avalanches for a number of reasons: a large volume of snow starts to slide all at one time, the usual settlement and loss of internal cohesion as the slide starts throws any but the best skier off balance, once downed the skier is inundated by succeeding waves of snow from above.

Hazard from soft-slab avalanches is at its highest during and immediately after storms, especially storms with a high precipitation rate and accompanied by wind. The duration of danger is dependent upon temperature and the snowpack structure; the warmer the temperature the faster slabs will stabilize.

Triggering of slabs by a skier or climber is the major cause of slab avalanche accidents. Although soft slabs may be triggered by the weight of the first person to cross the slope, harder slabs, being more unpredictable, may not release even after the passage of several skiers.

Fig. 4.10 This wet snow slab slid slowly for about a week until it gained sufficient speed to release. Some authorities call these type of slides transition avalanches or trans-avalanches for short. Keep away from such areas showing cracking and compression lines. Photo by Leon Kubbernus.

85

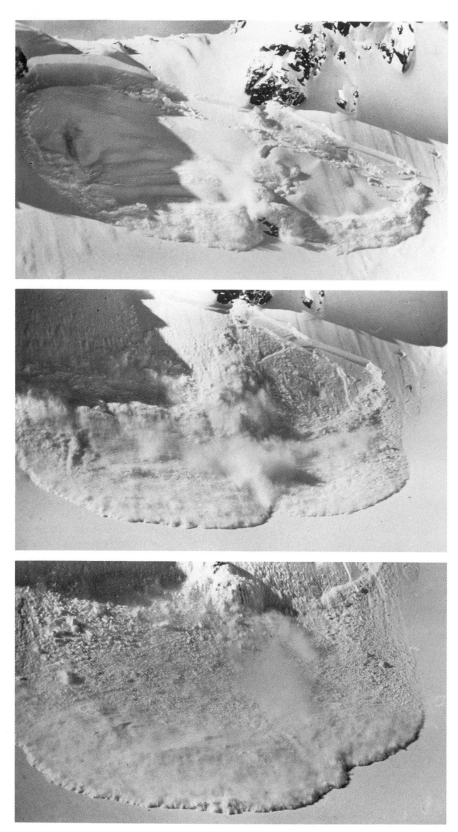

A soft slab avalanche releases from a facture line up to 4 m deep.

The slab disintegrates into powder as it gathers speed.

At the height of the avalanche, the flowing snow is accompanied by a cloud of snow dust. Photos by Tony Salway.

Fig. 4.12 Wet snow avalanche showing typical snowball-like appearance of the debris. Photo by Alf Skrastins.

How Slabs Fail

Dry-slab avalanches fail by shear in a weak layer which, in turn, produces a tensile failure at the crown, a shear fracture on the flanks and compressive failure at the stauch-wall. Cracking of the slab, when once it starts, is extremely rapid.

A weak layer in the snowpack has a certain strength depending upon cohesion or bond strength between crystals, and also upon static friction which varies with crystal type; the strength of the layer will vary with the texture of the snow. It's fairly obvious that large, poorly-bonded, depth hoar crystals form a much weaker layer than small well-bonded grains. When some triggering force destroys local cohesion, the crystals begin to move and friction passes from static friction to dynamic (moving) friction. If the slope is steeper than the angle of dynamic friction an avalanche will release. For any type of snow the angle of dynamic friction is smaller than that of static friction by about 10°. For example poorly-bonded depth hoar crystals are at their limit of equilibrium on a slope of 45°, but when once they begin to move they have an angle of dynamic friction of 35°.

Failure in Wet Snow

The mechanism for failure in wet snow is not completely understood. It was previously thought that wet snow avalanching only occurred when liquid water had penetrated snow and lubricated a sliding surface. While this is true in some cases, it has been found that in maritime climates some avalanching occurred long before water had penetrated very deeply into the snowpack. When the snowpack contained a buried layer of intricately shaped crystals, avalanching occurred as soon as the air temperature reached 0°C. In such climates, atmospheric warming and rain directly influence snowpack stability.

Movement of liquid water through snow is influenced by the structure of the snowpack. Coarse grained snow allows easy drainage and results in relatively stable snowpack. Fine grained snow inhibits drainage and leads to more rapid avalanching.

Saturated layers can occur at different depths within the snowpack. The strength of a saturated layer is often stronger than adjacent layers and avalanches release within the layer below the saturated layer, which often contains weak, cohesionless grains which have probably formed as a result of water seeping from the slushy layer above.

Size of Avalanches

Avalanches vary tremendously in size from small sluffs a few metres high to the giant avalanches of the Himalaya where millions of tonnes of snow fall many vertical kilometres.

Most of us need only consider two sizes of slide. The smallest slides, which only bring down a few cubic metres of snow and which are not large enough to bury a person are called **sluffs**. Even so, a small sluff is quite enough to dislodge a climber from a precarious position and carry him into danger. Mountaineer Frank Smythe, writing in "Kamet Conquered" about a sluff which carried him down a steep slope says:

"As an avalanche it was so small as to be scarcely worthy of the name, yet it had carried me helplessly down the slope and, had the fates not been kind, would have killed me. It is not the spectacular snow avalanche weighing tens of thousands of tons that causes mountaineering disasters, but the small, apparently inoffensive slide, that buries the mountaineer in the depth of a crevasse or casts him over a precipice."

Any slide which releases enough snow to bury you is considered to be an avalanche.

"There is no better example to illustrate the point that the small avalanches are often the killers. The snow ran for only 90 feet — yet it was able to bury the victim sufficient to suffocate her." So concludes the accident report about an accident in 1961 at Aspen Ski area, Colorado.

On Mount Foraker in Alaska, a 8 cm new-snow slab released on a sheet of blue ice and carried four climbers several thousand feet to their death.

Statistics show that a large proportion of back-country avalanche accidents involve relatively small slides which have been triggered by the victims themselves.

Fig. 4.13 The small slab avalanche at Aspen, which buried and killed skier, only ran for 30 m down a slope which many people would not consider dangerous. Photo courtesy Dale Gallagher, U.S. Forest Service.

Fig. 4.14 Large new snow soft slab avalanches on the Gaudergrat above Davos, Switzerland. Avalanching has occurred on almost all the slopes which are steep enough to slide. Photo by André Roch.

Slab avalanches with an average crown fracture line greater than 15 cm deep are potentially dangerous. The depth of fracture lines can vary from a few centimeters to over 10 metres; even in the relatively low-lying Cairngorms of Scotland crown fracture lines of 8 metres have been reported. The huge avalanche which killed 7 helicopter skiers in the Purcell Mountains of British Columbia on Valentine's Day in 1979 is reported to have had a fracture line which extended over a kilometre around the mountain and which, in places, was 3 metres deep. Sometimes crown fracture lines run for several kilometres around an entire mountain cirque.

One method, useful to both the amateur and to those engaged in avalanche control work, of classifying avalanches by size is shown in the adjacent table adapted from the original work of Dave McClung. Omitted from the table are typical impact pressures which range from 1 kPa to 1000 kPa.

Size of Avalanches			
Size	Description	Typical path length	Typical mass
1	Relatively harmless to people	10 m	10 t
2	Could bury, kill or injure a person	100 m	100 t
3	Could bury a car, destroy a small building or break a few trees.	1,000 m	1,000 t
4	Could destroy a railway car, large truck, several buildings or a forest with an area up to 4 hectares (40,000 m sq).	2,000 m	10,000 t
5	Largest snow avalanches known; could destroy a village or a forest of 40 hectares.	3,000 m	100,000 t

The Avalanche Path

The avalanche path is the entire area in which an avalanche moves. It has three parts:

Starting Zone

The starting zone is the area where unstable snow breaks loose from the snowcover and starts to slide. In the case of a slab avalanche this zone extends from the crown line to the stauchwall.

Track

The slope or channel down which snow moves at a more or less uniform speed is called the track. It may be non-existent in a small slab avalanche or, conversely, can extend for several kilometres in a very large snow slide.

Runout Zone

The runout zone is the portion of the avalanche path where snow slows down and comes to rest. The area where the bulk of the snow accumulates is called the **deposition zone**. Sometimes this is surrounded by an area of deposited air-borne snow dust called the **wind-blast zone**. In high mountains, where avalanche tracks are long and steep, you should be aware that runout zones can extend for considerable distances across relatively flat terrain.

Fig. 4.15 Avalanche path nomenclature.

Fig. 4.16 A massive avalanche which fell some 3000 m off the south face of Mount Logan and raced across the flat Icefield in front of Mount McArthur for a distance of about 1.5 km. Photo by Clair Israelson.

Avalanche Triggers

The most important natural trigger is the rapid loading of snow slopes by additional snowfall, rainfall or wind drifting of snow onto lee slopes. A sudden temperature rise will also cause increased stresses within the snowpack because snow is weaker and deforms more easily at higher temperatures and because temperature induced pressure changes within the snowpack may result in a weakening of the bond between ice grains. Long cold periods allow recrystallization to take place, further reducing the strength of loose weak layers. Other natural triggers are small sluffs of loose-snow, snow falling off trees, falling cornices and occasionally earthquakes.

Artificial triggers can be explosives or sonic booms, but most commonly it is the additional weight of a skier or climber on the snow surface which add sufficient stress to the snow to allow the slide to releases.

On a few occasions it's been suspected that vibration from a passing helicopter has been the final catalyst. There's the story of the four Irishmen in Scotland which has elements of farce but no happy ending. It really began when a climber fell from the Carn Mor Dearg - Ben Nevis arete and was taken to the CIC hut to be picked up by helicopter. As the helicopter was coming in, it passed just below a group of four climbers who were taking a stroll around the bottom of Carn Dearg to look at some ice. They had no intention of climbing that day; heavy snowfalls, followed by strong winds and a thaw had made conditions too dangerous. As the helicopter passed, they stopped to dig out their cameras from their packs; here was a chance to get a photograph of the chopper

Fig. 4.17 Helicopters are widely used for avalanche control and rescue. In extremely unstable conditions it is possible that the vibration is sufficient to trigger avalanches. Photo by Chris Stethem.

when it returned. At that moment, a huge slab avalanche, the largest ever seen on Ben Nevis — the debris covered an area 150 metres by 250 metres — broke from Castle Gullies and Raeburn Buttress and swept them away down a rocky hillside. It was so unexpected; the noise of the helicopter had effectively masked any sound the avalanche may have made. Two of the climbers suffering minor injuries came to rest on the surface and were able to dig out a third companion with a fractured skull. Evacuation was speedy: the helicopter on its return journey was waved down and another three casualties put aboard. The fourth man wasn't found for three days; he had landed in a gully and had died instantly of a broken neck.

Fig. 4.18 An ice avalanche falls onto the popular route
leading to Bow Hut in the Canadian Rockies. The skiers
in the foreground, overtaken by the dust cloud, were out
of range of the debris which stopped just short of the
leader of the party. Photos by Kevin Cronin.

Climax Avalanches

Climax avalanches bring down the accumulation of several snowfalls or, even the whole of the seasons snowpack right down to the ground. They are usually the result of a significant change in the weather such as a warming trend or additional snowfall. Early season climax cycles are difficult to predict. Learn to recognize weather conditions which might lead to instability and keep off steep slopes at such times. Most climax cycles occur in spring when the whole snowpack, or significant layers of it, become isothermal. Isothermal means equal temperature throughout. In avalanche terminology the term **isothermal slides** refers to slides which occur when a layer of snow becomes isothermal at a temperature of close to 0°C. The first occasion in spring when temperatures remain above freezing for several days and nights is the time to be wary. Keep an eye on indicator slopes —those which get the greatest amount of radiation — for the first sign of avalanching. If you think a cycle of climax avalanching is about to occur it's best to stay out of the mountains until conditions improve.

Ice Avalanches

As a glacier flows down a steep uneven slope, it often splits open into a chaotic zone of crevasses and unstable ice blocks many metres high called seracs. Although it's the movement of the glacier which causes the seracs to topple, air temperature changes and internal melting within the seracs play a part too; it appears that ice avalanches are more active during the late afternoon. Because of their unpredictability, ice avalanches are extremely dangerous. The photographs on the opposite page show an ice avalanche mixed with powder snow falling over a cliff onto a well travelled route leading to the Bow Hut on the Wapta Icefields (Canadian Rockies). Although it looks as if the skiers are about to be overwhelmed, they were only caught in the accompanying cloud of snow dust and not engulfed by the avalanche itself. A party of 6 guides and 23 climbers on Mount Rainier were less lucky. While stopped in a supposedly safe place near Disappointment Cleaver, part of the icefall created by the junction of the Ingraham and Emmons Glaciers broke away and came sweeping down to bury 11 victims under 20 metres of car-sized blocks.

So what can you do to minimize the danger? Your only defence is to move fast and don't stop until clear of danger. On no account camp below an area of seracs on a glacier or below a cliff topped with an ice wall.

Fig. 4.19 An ice avalanche off the Jungfraujoch carves a curved path in wet snow. Photo by André Roch.

5

Observing Snow Conditions

In previous chapters you've learned about terrain and what effect a change of weather has on the snowpack. Now you are ready to put on your skis and learn something of the practical aspects of snowcraft.

The professional snow scientist has many techniques at his fingertips using equipment not available to the winter traveller who must improvise with equipment normally carried on a trip such as skis, poles, a shovel and maybe an avalanche probe and snow saw. For instance, ski poles and a shovel can be substituted for the Ramsonde, a device for measuring the relative hardness of various snow layers. Many of the tests have been developed by professionals. Like them you will cut out a column of snow and do a shovel test to look for sliding layers. You will use the hand test to estimate the density of different layers of snow in the wall of a snowpit, and finish with a Rutschblock test to get an indication of snow stability.

Fig. 5.1 Observation is the key to safe winter travel. Signs of previous avalanche activity such as sluffs or snowballs rolling down a slope all contribute to your assessment of snow stability. Photo by Roland V. Emetaz, courtesy U.S. Forest Service.

Observation

Observation is the key to safe travel in avalanche terrain — observation not only of the mountain scenery but of the multitude of clues indicating snow conditions visible to the perceptive traveller. Some of the things you should look for are as follows:

Evidence of Avalanching

This is the most important clue to instability you are likely to be given. Use other slopes in the area as indicator slopes. If nearby slopes have avalanched observe how much snow has come down, how far the slides have run and the depth of the fracture line if they are slab avalanches.

In particular look for recent avalanches on slopes of similar aspect to those you wish to cross. New snow sluffing off cliffs or snowballs rolling down steep slopes are either an indication of settling and strengthening of the snowpack or of isothermal conditions developing.

Wind Direction

You must always be aware of the direction from which the wind has been blowing and its approximate strength. Snow blowing off ridges, cornices, rime, drifts around rocks and trees are all good indicators. As a general rule the more pronounced the feature the stronger the wind. Knowledge of wind direction and strength will enable you to decide if you are on a lee slope and likely to encounter slab. Refer to the section on determining wind direction in the chapter "Recognizing Avalanche Terrain".

Aspect

The aspect of a slope to both sun and wind is most important. If you've ventured onto a lee slope look for layers of soft or hard slab. On a spring ski tour watch the shadows; when they point to a slope like a warning finger the slope is receiving the maximum amount of heat. In depth hoar country, a north slope may consist of little but loose highly unstable sugar snow crystals early in the winter.

Fig. 5.2 Snowballs rolling down the slope is evidence that the surface layers of the snow are warming up. The convex, V-shaped channels were caused by rain a few days previously.

Fig. 5.3 Leaning trees indicate that creep is occurring in the snowpack and that the slope is a potential avalanche slope. Slides in the background reinforce this observation. Photo by Alf Skrastins.

The Snow Surface

Observe the texture of the snow surface and note any changes. Is it just a local effect caused by wind or are you on a slope of different aspect? Look for wind or sun crusts, surface hoar, riming or convex furrows which are signs of rain. Some snow surface features like etching and rippling indicate previous wind direction.

Etching forms beautiful parallel lines on a hard snow surface. The steep edge of the lines faces the direction from which the wind was blowing.

Rippling A light wind causes rippling of the snow surface by a process of sorting particles of different sizes on the ground. Smaller particles are picked up and deposited on the lee side of larger ones, thus promoting the formation of tiny mounds which eventually grow a few centimetres in height. Examination of a rippled snow surface will show that the shallower side of the ripples faces the wind.

One difficulty in determining the direction of wind from ripples is that once the snow has hardened there is little free snow on the surface and so the formation of ripples stops. If the wind continues, erosion begins and changes the appearance of the ripples by cutting into the shallow windward side and depositing snow on the lee side, thus reversing the shape. The only guide you have as to which process is taking place is to test the hardness of the snow surface. Soft, powdery snow is probably forming ripples, while hard, compact ripples are probably being eroded.

Form Widespread areas of slab can often be recognized from a distance by the smooth rounded form the terrain assumes. Look for and learn to recognize such areas. It's interesting to note that in hard slab the grains of snow tend to be all one size thus inhibiting the initiation of rippling.

Cracks Glide of the snowpack over the ground may form cracks in the surface which should be taken as a warning sign of passible isothermal slides. In spring, such cracks may widen over a period of time before avalanching occurs.

In cold snow, cracks running ahead of your skis are a sure sign that you are standing on slab; an important warning of instability which must not be ignored.

Fig. 5.4 Beware when the snow cracks and settles around you. Photo by Gillean Daffern.

Feel of Snow Under Skis

With experience it's possible to assess snow conditions by feeling changes in consistency as your skis slide through the snow.

Change in the Type of Snow

Learn to recognize when you go from one type of snow to another. Sometimes there's no visible indication, but the snow will just feel different. If you're using waxes you may suddenly find you are slipping, or that your skis are balling up so you can't glide as easily. Perhaps trail breaking becomes either easier or harder. Why has the snow changed? There are many answers; think about them and try to decide the reason which fits your present circumstances.

Settling

One feeling which everyone will recognize once it has been experienced is the scary sinking feeling as slabs sink underfoot. Sometimes this is a gentle subsidence, sensed rather than felt; a slight settling which produces no visible signs at the snow surface. This is a sure indication of soft slab. If you're on a steep slope when the settling occurs you'll be relieved to know that the snow has settled without avalanching. But ten paces on it may avalanche rather than settle. It's your decision; retreat or risk it.

As snow slabs become harder, settlement will be more pronounced and you will actually feel the drop. There will be an audible "whumph" and often some visible sign of settlement on the snow surface such as dishing or cracking.

Hard Slab

Once experienced hard slab has a recognizable feel to it. It usually feels harder than windcrust and the surface has a sort of smooth velvety texture. In some instances the point of a ski pole won't be able to penetrate the surface. Sometimes it will have a hollow feeling, especially high in the mountains where depth hoar actually creates a space below the slab leaving it unsupported. On Bridger Peak, Montana, a ski tour leader led his party off a dangerous slope about 15 seconds before it slid. *"In spite of the fact that initial testing had given no warning of hazard conditions the party leader became increasingly worried about slab avalanches as the party progressed. He later said that he sensed a kind of 'hollow feeling' to the snow."* After-the-fact probing indicated a metre and a half slab with 0.3 metres of depth hoar underneath which the initial shallow probing had failed to reveal. Failure of such dangerous slabs is dramatic; the sudden jolting drop accompanied by an audible cracking of the surface which may extend for a considerable distance across the slope.

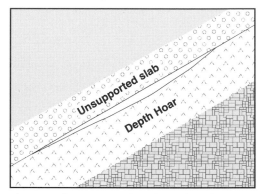

Fig. 5.5 Depth Hoar may settle under hard slab leaving a space several centimetres deep. Such slabs have a characteristic hollow feeling to them.

Movement of Skis

The way in which your skis move through the snow is another indication of snow conditions. If your skis tend to skid sideways you may be on crust, hard slab or ice. If your skis subside gently into the snow as you break trail, but are hard to push forward or lift out, you are probably skiing in soft slab. When your skis or crampons ball up in new or settling snow it's an indication of a rise in temperature. Consider how much the temperature is rising and the effect it might have on the stability of the snowpack.

Ski Tracks

You can learn a lot by observing your tracks: how much the snow has consolidated, its moisture content, and whether you are straying into an area of hard or soft slab.

How Far your Skis Sink

If your skis don't sink in at all then you're either skiing on hard slab, wind or sun crust, or on ice. On a side slope skis will tend to slip sideways, pushing off any loose surface snow. A glance at the tracks will soon ascertain if you are on ice, but the difference between hard slab and windcrust is rather more difficult to decide. Both wind crust and sun crust, providing the surface is not obscured by fresh snow, exhibit some form of erosion, deposition or uneven melting. Slab, particularly harder slab, is usually quite smooth and deposited in distinctive rounded, drift-like shapes with gentle contours. If you find your skis always sinking in to the same depth you should suspect wind slab. On the other hand, if the surface consists of alternating breakable and hard crust you are probably on consolidated wind-blown snow.

Try to relate the depth to which the skis sink to the total depth of the most recent snowfall. For instance, if there has been a 30 cm snowfall and the skis sink in only 5 cm then the snow is well consolidated; it has either undergone rounding or been formed into slab. If, however, you sink to a depth of 20 cm then little settlement has occurred and conditions may still be very dangerous.

In practice it appears that the potentially dangerous types of snow are those which produce unusually hard or unusually soft layers in the snowpack. Obviously, if you are sinking in up to your thighs there is a large enough quantity of unconsolidated snow to give an avalanche of devastating proportions.

Appearance

Good snow at a moderate temperature packs evenly into firm ski tracks. The sides cut down cleanly and hold together without the snow collapsing onto the bottom of the trail. This is a sign that metamorphism is taking place and that the snow has strengthened. If the snow collapses from the sides onto the bottom of the trail and appears sparkling, almost crystalline, then you are probably skiing through recrystallized snow.

Soft slab may be indicated if blocks slide out between your skis — the second skier in line will often notice this — or if your skis start slipping sideways or backwards on easy grades.

Fig. 5.6 Suspect soft slab when blocks break up between your skis.

Icy or wet tracks are the result of MF-metamorphism. The snowpack should be examined to see how far down the snow is melting. Free water on the surface is a sign of dangerous thaw conditions in the mountains, meaning that the whole depth of the snowpack is probably close to 0°C. Keep off any slope of 15° or more if these conditions occur.

When breaking trail in cold dry climates, particularly early in the season, there'll be times when you break right through to the ground. In most cases you'll find a layer of depth hoar at the bottom of the snowpack.

Kick Turns

When climbing a steep slope using kick turns, note the behavior of the snow at each turn. Does a wedge of snow slide out and if so how thick is it? Is any snow being pulled from above? Where is the sliding layer? Is there more than one sliding layer? Is the snow of the same consistency each time you turn? You may well be in firm consolidated snow at one end of a traverse and in slab at the other.

Ski testing

Slope stability may be evaluated by ski testing. This potentially dangerous practice is not recommended for the amateur. The main argument against using this method of evaluation in the backcountry is that test skiing is rarely conclusive; one pass by a test skier is not necessarily an indication that a slope is safe. Avalanches can start by progressive failure of support within the snow. The slope may fail after the third or fourth skier has crossed safely.

Any test skiing should be done very cautiously on very small slopes of the same aspect. Take all precautions. Use transceivers and always have someone watching you from a safe place.

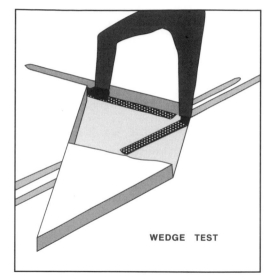

WEDGE TEST

Fig. 5.7 Watch the snow on the inside corner of a kick turn. Does it break loose as a cohesive slab?

Fig. 5.8 The best way to learn snowcraft is with an experienced instructor.

Ski Pole Test

Use

The ski pole test is a means of checking snow layers in the top metre or so of the snowpack. It consists of pushing the pole into the surface at a controlled rate and feeling the changes in resistance as various snow layers are encountered. Although used to check for specific indications of hazard such as hard slab and depth hoar, it should never be used as the sole judge of snow stability, but rather as an indication that snow conditions have changed and that further testing is desirable.

Limitations

This test has a number of limitations: it's impossible to penetrate more than a few centimetres into heavy wet snow, the length of a ski pole and an arm limits the total depth which can be probed, and finally, the ski pole test will not confirm soft slab, although it will give an indication that slab might exist. If soft slab is suspected it must be backed by other tests.

Where to Test

Ski pole tests should be carried out regularly in avalanche terrain; often a seconds pause is enough to detect a significant change in the snow. Before venturing onto a large slope test a small slope of the same aspect first, making sure the elevation is as close as possible to the estimated trigger zone of the larger slope.

The Test

Always test at right angles to the snow surface. Using the basket end first, push the pole smoothly into the snow with just enough pressure to overcome the resistance. Try not to force or jerk the pole down. Too much pressure and you'll lurch through the snowpack without feeling anything. If the snow is too hard, reverse the pole and use the handle end, making sure before you start that you don't have loose grips. Push in as far as possible, down to the ground if the snowpack is shallow or to arms length if the snow is soft enough.

Once you've made the hole withdraw the pole slowly, letting the basket press against the side of the hole. This way the hard and soft layers can be felt. Another technique for examining snow layers is to move the handle in a circle to form a cone-shaped hole in the snow. In this way you can examine the top 30 centimetres.

If you need to know the total depth of the snowpack use a sectional avalanche probe. Generally though, the tourer is only concerned with the top metre or two of the snowpack.

Fig. 5.9 When conducting a ski pole test always push in the pole at right angles to the snow.

Interpreting resistance

Little resistance Unsettled new snow, depth hoar or new soft slab.

Stiff Well settled snow, firm windcrust or soft slab.

Hard Compacted snow, medium slab or windcrust. Handle end will have to be used.

Very hard Hard slab. Point of ski pole will hardly mark the surface.

Ideal situation Steadily increasing resistance with depth and no very hard or very soft layers.

Wet snow Packs tight in the hole preventing the ski pole from being pushed in more than a few centimetres.

Sudden breakthrough Probably a layer of depth hoar. Check several places in the area to obtain an average depth.

Very hard and very soft layers Any thin layers which are very hard or very soft in the top 2 m of the snowpack should be investigated further. Read the remainder of this chapter to learn how to do the Shovel Shear test, the Rutschblock test and the Loaded Column test.

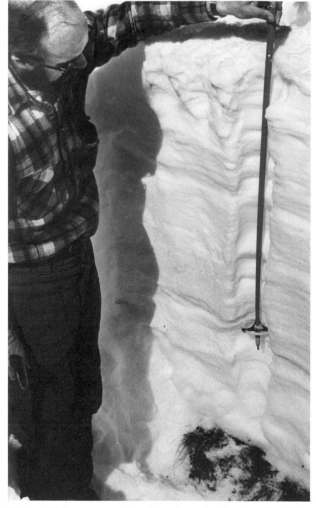

Fig. 5.10 This cut-away section shows the typical layering of a cold shallow snowpack. Note where the depth hoar has collapsed away from the settled snow near the bottom. Photo by Gillean Daffern.

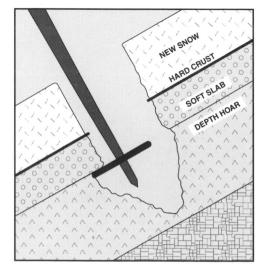

Fig. 5.11 By drawing the basket against the side of the hole, it is easy to feel the hard layers. The thickness of the depth hoar can be estimated by feeling the underside of the settled snow above.

Shovel Shear Test

This important test is used to locate and identify weak layers of snow or a weak interface between layers within the snowpack, and to gauge the additional loading required to initiate failure. It is the best, and probably the only way, to identify buried surface hoar layers and should always be used if other observations such as ski pole tests indicate that a sliding layer might be present.

However, the shovel shear test is not a good test for determining the stability of the snowpack. Many a good ski trip has been ruined by relying solely on the results of this test.

The shovel shear test must be done on a slope with the same orientation as the potential avalanche slope and as close to the elevation of the trigger zone as possible.

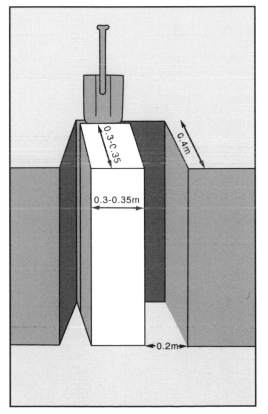

Fig. 5.12 Recommended dimensions for the shovel shear test. In practice you will approximate in terms of the width of your shovel.

Method

The following procedure is suggested for use in the back country.

1. First of all probe to determine the total depth of the snowpack and to get an idea of the layering. By doing so you can find out the extent of thick layers of potential slab and any weak layers underneath.

2. Dig a snow pit about 1 metre wide and as deep as you think necessary from knowledge gained from other observations. It should be at least as deep as the most recent snowfall, with a practical maximum of about 1.5 m. Observe the layering of the snow as you dig, especially the hardness, crystal type and free water content of significant layers.

3. Trim the uphill wall of the pit so that it's vertical.

4. Excavate a chimney in the uphill wall about a shovel's width wide and just over a shovel's width into the hill.

5 . Mark on the snow surface a square block with sides 30 cm to 35 cm (a wide shovel's width) at the side of the chimney.

6. Using a snow saw or the tail of a ski cut out a triangle of snow at the other side of the block.

7. Make a vertical cut at the back of the block about 0.7 m (2 shovel widths) deep or, if you have an indication of the depth of a weak layer, cut down to just below the suspected layer. Do not cut all the way to the bottom to start with and do not cut down into depth hoar or the block will collapse.

8. Carefully insert the shovel to its full depth at the back of the block, then using both hands and without levering pull gently on the shovel handle. Cut down the back of the block another 0.5 m and repeat the test.

9. If a significant sliding layer is present the block will shear off in a smooth even plane. If the block doesn't slide off smoothly the test is invalid and must be repeated.

10. Examine the fracture surface and try to deter mine type and size of the snow crystals causing the sliding layer.

Fig. 5.13 Shear from failure during a shovel test. In this case, the block slid on a thin hard key layer —probably a sun crust. Photo by Gillean Daffern.

Interpretation of Results

The primary reason for doing a shovel shear test is to identify weak layers or lack of bond between adjacent layers within the snowpack. It is possible, with experience, to estimate the strength of shear of the weak layer or interface. However any estimation of the shear strength should only be used as an indication of the need for further testing.

If the block slides during cutting or insertion of the shovel then obviously there is a very weak sliding layer present. If there is a significant depth of snow above the sliding layer you should be looking for other signs of instability in the area and should be very wary of skiing steep slopes. Continue testing down the block looking for other weak layers.

If the block slides off with pressure from the shovel — remember it must exhibit a clean, smooth shear to be valid — and if there is more than 15 cm of snow above the sliding layer, a Rutschblock Test is certainly indicated.

It is not uncommon in cold dry climates with a shallow snowpack for the block to collapse into the depth hoar layer as it is cut. In this case, you must decide if the overlying snow structure is strong enough to support itself over the top of the depth hoar. If you have any doubts about the strength of the snow above the depth hoar try the Compression Test described below.

Compression Test

Use this test if you suspect slab and where there's a layer of depth hoar at the bottom of a shallow snowpack.

Proceed as for the Shovel Test, but do not cut into the back of the block. Cut the sides down into any depth hoar layer. Now place the shovel flat on the top of the block and bear down in an attempt to break the cantilevered slab and collapse the layers underneath.

The force required for failure will give you an indication of both the ease of collapse of a depth hoar layer and the strength of the slab. Slab strength is a most important factor in an early season snowpack underlain by depth hoar.

Fig. 5.14 The Compression Test is used if you suspect slab and where there's a layer of depth hoar at the bottom of a shallow snowpack.

Rutschblock Test

This entertaining and instructional test is used to identify weak layers in the snowpack and as an indicator of snow stability. If you only do one test in a snowpit, this is the one to do. It will give you the most pertinent and reliable information. Because you are using a much larger block (about a ski length square), careful selection of the test site is necessary for reliable results. Probe to avoid logs, brush, rocks, etc. before digging the pit.

Method

1. Select a site as close as possible to the slope you wish to ski, and of the same aspect. If you must do this test on slopes of less than 30°, the lower wall should be as smooth as possible, and a second person should watch for small displacements (less than 1 cm) that indicate shear failure.
2. Dig a pit and completely isolate a block about 2 m wide (a ski length) by 1.5 m deep using a combination of shovel, snow saw, ski tail, or knotted rope; whichever is the quickest. Flare the side cuts a little so that the block is free to slide out.
3. Load the block in the following sequence and observe when a clean fracture takes place.

Loading steps

1. The block slides as it is being cut out.
2. Put skis on and carefully approach the block from above. Step down with one ski onto the block close to the upper wall. Transfer your weight carefully and place the other ski on the block.
3. Flex your knees quickly, without lifting your heels, to transfer your weight to the snow, thus compacting the surface layers.
4. Jump up and land on the same compacted spot near the back of the block with both skis.
5. Jump onto the same spot a second time.
6. Either jump on the same spot on the block without skis or repeat steps 3 & 4 with skis on, landing in the middle of the block.

Variations of the Rutschblock have been developed for snowboarders (Shredblock) and snowmobilers. Take an avalanche safety course to learn about them.

Fig. 5.15 Rutschblock Test showing good displacement. Note the position of the skier near the back of the block. In this case the side walls were exposed by shovelling. Photo by Mark Shubin

Interpretation of results.

Conservative backcountry skiers will not ski a slope if the Rutschblock test fails with less than 2 jumps (stop 5 or earlier).

If the snow fails at any time before you jump on the block, instability is considered to be high on slopes of similar aspect and steepness.

If it fails when you jump on the snow with skis on, local instability should be suspected on similar slopes.

If you have to jump on the block with skis off or jump on the middle of the block to get failure, or if there is no failure, there is a low risk of avalanches.

Limitations

The Rutschblock test will not identify weak layers above the layer penetrated by your skis during the test. For instance, if you sink 20 cm into the surface snow when you step onto the block, a weak layer at 15 cm may not be apparent. The test has been found to be most effective on slopes greater than 30°.

Other Stability Tests

Over the past few years there have been attempts to develop more reliable stability tests that can be easily done in the backcountry with minimal equipment, but that will give consistent results when done by different people in different locations. Two of these deserve mention: The "Tap" test developed in Canada and the "Stuffblock" test developed in Montana, USA.

Tap test

The advantage of this test is that it only requires a shovel and so can be done by snowboarders and snowmobilers as well as skiers.

1. Isolate a column as for the Shovel Shear test, but for this test, cut the back of the column right down to the bottom and flatten the top of the column.

2. Place a shovel blade on top of the column and tap 10 times with the fingertips flexing the hand at the wrist. Failures up to this point are *easy*.

3. Tap from the elbow 10 times. Any failure is *moderate*. Finally hit the shovel with open hand or fist 10 times and rate any failure as *hard*.

Stuffblock test

While this test requires more equipment, it gives the most consistent results.

1. Isolate a column as for the Tap test above.

2. Fill a stuff sack with 4.5 kg (10 lbs.) of snow as weighed with a lightweight scale. Place a shovel on top of the column and the stuff bag on top. Any failure is *easy*.

3. Using a short length of cord attached to the bottom of the stuff sack and marked at 10 cm intervals, drop the bag onto the shovel from a height of 10 cm. Repeat at 20 cm. Any failure is still *easy*.

4. Repeat at 10 cm intervals. Any failure at 30 - 50 cm is considered *moderate* and above 50 cm is *hard*.

Remember that the above tests only provide one piece of the information you need to make an informed decision on stability.

Snowpits

There are two reasons for backcountry skiers to dig a snowpit: to get a quick look at the composition of the snowpack while doing a few stability related tests, and to make a detailed examination of the snowpack for educational or record-keeping purposes.

Few skiers have either the time or the energy to make a detailed snowpit examination during a day trip. If you're staying in one area for several days, however, it's a worthwhile exercise because it gives you definitive information on the state of the snowpack. You can compile a snow profile by making certain observations of the snowpack. The form of snow profile useful in the backcountry is known as a **hasty pit**.

The objective is to identify weak layers in the snowpack and assess their strength, to obtain snow temperatures if you suspect the snow is close to 0°C, to determine the progress of metamorphism and to find the depth of potential slab avalanches. You need only collect information that is most significant for stability at the time of the observation.

Where to Dig

Like all other tests on snow, the snowpit should be dug on a small slope of similar orientation to a potential avalanche slope and as close to the trigger zone as possible. The farther away from the release zone you dig the snowpit, the less relevant the information obtained will be. You can waste a lot of time digging snowpits in locations that are not representative of the slope you wish to ski.

The best place to dig is in the middle of an open slope, away from trees. Probe the site quickly to avoid buried brush or rocks and to make sure you are not digging in old avalanche debris. Avoid ridges or the lee side of obstructions where the wind may have altered the composition of the snowpack.

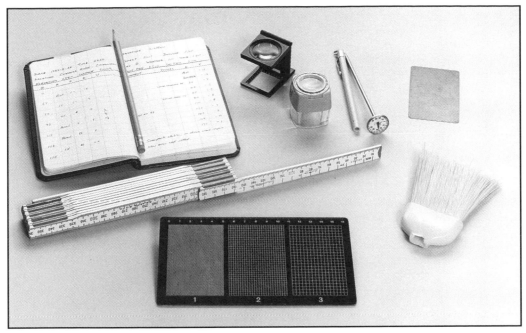

Fig. 5.16 In order to make the effort of digging a snow pit worthwhile some additional equipment is necessary.

Recording Observations

There are a number of books on the market for recording snowpit observations. The better ones use water-resistant paper. A suitable format for recording observations is shown on page 109 along with the symbols used. Make a copy of this page to take with you on your trip. Record the results for later study.

Procedure

1. Using a probe or ski pole check the depth of the snow and try to identify, by feel, the location of weak layers. If probing indicates that the pit to be dug on a particular site will reach the ground, make sure you're not standing over rocks or tree stumps. Determine the new snow depth.

2. Record date, time, location and elevation of the snowpit site in the spaces provided at the top of the page.

3. Observe the surface of the snow and note the surface roughness according to the following criteria:

Surface Roughness	
Symbol	**Class**
———	Smooth
∿	Wavy (rippled)
‿‿‿	Concave furrows (sun cups)
⌒⌒⌒	Convex furrows (rain channels)
∿∿	Random furrows (drifts, sastrugi)

4. Note the type of snow on the surface.

Surface Snow	
Symbol	Description
ØD	Loose dry snow
ØW	Loose wet snow
=	Wind crust
~	Crust from melting, sun, or rain
v	Surface hoar

5. Record aspect and incline of terrain as close as you can judge it. Some compasses have a built-in clinometer or you can use a slope meter such as the Life Link model illustrated on page 116.

6. Note the weather and record type of precipitation and cloud cover using symbols or longhand. If you know the hourly rate of snowfall record the actual amount using, for example, *2 to indicate 2 cm per hour.

Precipitation Type & Intensity		
Class	Symbol	Description
No precipitation	NIL	
Light Snow	*L or *-1	Continuous fall that accumulates at a rate of 1 cm per hour or less.
Moderate snow	*M or *2 for 2 cm	Snow accumulates at a rate of 1 cm - 3 cm per hour.
Heavy snow	*H	Snow accumulates at a rate of more than 3 cm per hour.
Very light rain	VLR	
Light rain	LR	Accumulation of up to 3 mm of water per hour.
Moderate rain	MR	Accumulation of 3 mm to 8 mm of water per hour.
Heavy rain	HR	Accumulation of 8 mm of water per hour or more.
Freezing rain	FR	
Mixed snow & rain	*R	

Cloud Cover		
Class	Symbol	Description
Clear	◯	No clouds.
Partly cloudy	◐	Clouds cover half or less of the sky.
Cloudy	◑	Broken clouds; more than half but not all of the sky is covered.
Overcast	⊕	Sky is completely covered.
Obscured	⊗	Clouds not discernable; mist or falling snow.

7. Record the air temperature, in the shade about a metre above the ground (hang your thermometer from the top of your ski pole). Note the temperature of the snow surface. Record also if the temperature is steady, or if it appears to be rising or falling. Although you probably won't have any means of measuring humidity, you should note if the air appears to be particularly humid.

8. Note direction from which wind blows using 8 major compass points — N, NE, E, SE, S, SW, W, NW.

Wind Direction & Strength		
Class	km/h	Description
Calm	0	No air in motion. Smoke rises vertically.
Light	1 - 25	Light to gentle breeze, twigs in motion
Moderate	26 - 40	Fresh breeze; small trees sway. Snow begins to drift.
Strong	> 40	Strong breeze and gale; whole trees in motion; snow drifting.

9. Record foot penetration by stepping into undisturbed snow and gently putting your body weight on one foot. The amount you sink in is an indication of the amount of unconsolidated snow, and if you know the amount of new snow penetration can be related to the rate of settlement.

10. Measure the depth of your ski tracks at a point where your weight has been on one ski and record in centimetres.

11. You are now ready to dig the pit. It should be dug with vertical faces and as deep as you have time for. In a generally well compacted snowpack you may only want to examine the top metre of snow but in a shallow snowpack you should always dig down to the ground. With the shovel clean off a smooth, plane face for examination; in steep terrain it's often best to use a side wall. Try to avoid having direct sunlight fall on the face you wish to examine.

SNOW PIT RECORD

Date:			Time:			Observer:			

Location:		Aspect:	Incline:

Elevation:		Sky:	Precip:	Wind:

Surface Roughness:		Foot Penetr:	Ski Penetr:

H (cm)	R	F	D (mm)	W	Shovel	Comment	H (cm)	T (°C)
							Air	
							Surface	

Evaluation of Stability:

CRYSTAL TYPES

New snow	+
New snow, rimed	+r
Graupel	⚊
Partially settled	/\
Rounded grains	●
Faceted crystals	□
Depth hoar	Λ
Melt-freeze particles	O
Surface hoar	V

SIZE OF CRYSTAL

Very Fine	0 - 0.5 mm
Fine	0.5 - 1 mm
Medium	1 - 2 mm
Coarse	2 - 4 mm
Very Coarse	4 mm or >

PRECIPITATION

No precipitation	Nil
Light snow	*L
Moderate snow	*M
Heavy snow	*H
Very light rain	VLR
Light rain	LR
Moderate rain	MR
Heavy rain	HR
Freezing rain	FR
Mixed rain/snow	*R

CLOUD COVER

Clear	◯
Partly cloudy	◑
Cloudy	◐
Overcast	⊕
Obscured	⊗

SURFACE ROUGHNESS

Smooth	———
Wavy	∿
Concave furrows	⌇
Convex furrows	∿
Random furrows	∿

HARDNESS

Very soft	FIST
Soft	4F
Medium	1F
Hard	P
Very hard	K
Ice	ICE

SURFACE SNOW

Loose dry snow
Loose wet snow
Wind crust
Sun/rain crust
Surface hoar

WATER CONTENT

Dry
Moist
Wet
Very wet
Slush

WIND

Calm
Light
Moderate
Strong

Fig. 5.17 An Instructor uses the hand test to evaluate the hardness of various layers.

Fig. 5.18 Run a credit card down through the snowpack to locate the top of thin hard layers. Run up from below to locate the bottom of the layer.

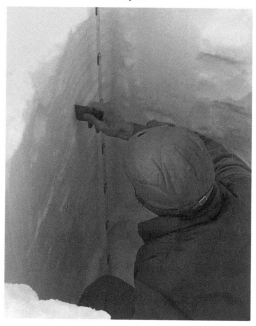

Examining the Snowpack

On examining the layered composition of the snowpack, some layers will be immediately apparent from visual inspection. Lightly flicking a woolen glove across the snow face, or better still brushing with a paintbrush, will etch out the hard and soft layers more clearly. In some areas where the snow is deep you may find a great many layers which reflect minor variations in wind, temperature or humidity. Remember, you are only concerned with layers that are unusually hard and unusually soft.

1. In warm conditions (close to 0°C) find the temperature of the snow. You are looking for snow which is within a degree or two of freezing point. This is the layer which might slide as a wet snow avalanche. Look in particular for clusters of large wet incohesive ice grains which indicate the advanced stage of MF-metamorphism (commonly called rotten snow). Ice lenses are caused by melt water percolating through the snowpack and freezing in the colder layer underneath. While their presence doesn't necessarily mean the snowpack is in a weak condition — in fact it may be very strong if well frozen — the chance of wet snow avalanching increases as the temperature of the snow around the ice approaches 0°C.

2. Determine the location of the various layers. Look for thin hard layers such as windcrust and suncrust, for very soft layers such as buried surface hoar, and for thick layers which are significantly harder or softer than the rest of the snowpack. Run a credit card vertically up and down the face of the snow to find the thin hard layers. Examine the bottom of the snowpack for depth hoar and try to assess how strong that layer is. Look also for granular crystals above suncrust or windcrust.

    Record the depth of each major layer boundary by measuring down from the surface and enter it in the first column (H for Height) on every second line.

3. Observe the hardness of each layer by using the hand test and enter it in the second column (R for Resistance) between the appropriate depths. Make a note under "comments" of any unusually hard or soft layers or of any obvious sliding planes. The hand test is accomplished by pushing various objects horizontally into the snow with moderate effort.

Fig. 5.20 When using the hand test, record the object which can be pushed into a snow layer with moderate effort. In this photograph, four gloved fingers indicate a relatively soft layer.

Hardness of Deposited Snow

Term	Order of magnitude of strength	Hand test	Entry
Very low	0 - 1,000	Fist in glove	FIST
Low	1,000 - 10,000	4 fingers in glove	4F
Medium	10,000 - 1000,000	1 finger in glove	1F
High	100,000 - 1,000,000	Pencil	P
Very High	> 1,000,000	Knife blade	K
Ice			ICE

Fig. 5.19 Field notes of a pit dug at the start of a week's ski mountaineering. It is important to record your opinion of the snowpack's stability and any other relevant factors.

SNOW PIT RECORD

Date: 82 - 2 - 22 Time: 0920
Observer: Daffern

Location: Cummins Ridge - Clemenceau
Aspect: E   Incline: Flat

Elevation: 6900' (2100 m)
Sky: ① Precip.: Nil Wind: Light N.W

Surface Roughness: Smooth
Foot Penetr.: 35 cm   Ski Penetr.: 9 cm

H (cm)	R	F	D(mm)	W	Shovel	Comment	H (cm)	T (°C)
0							Air	– 11
	Fist	⁄ ＼	0.5				Surface	– 12
27					Moderate	45 cm	20	– 7
	1F	⁄ ＼	0.3				40	– 7
70				⅄			60	– 7
	4F	●	0.5		Hard	74 cm	80	– 8
92				⌇			100	– 8
	P	●	0.5			Crust @ 98cm	120	– 7
117				⅋			140	– 5
	P	▱	0.5				175	– 1
152								
	1F	▱	1.0					
175						Ground		
No evidence of recent avalanching						Snowpack stable, no obvious weak layers New snow settling well.		

4. Using a magnifying glass and crystal screen, classify the shape of the grains in each layer and at the snow surface. Use the following graphic symbols to enter the shape in the third column (F for Form). Symbols can be mixed if several grain types are present in equal numbers, otherwise classify according to the majority of grains present.

Grain Types		
Class	Symbol	Description
New snow	+	Original shape is well recognizable.
New snow, rimed	+r	New snow crystals covered with rime.
Graupel	Ӿ	Heavily rimed crystals; original form is not recognizable.
Partially settled	/ \	The elements of the new snow are still recognizable; an intermediate stage between new snow and rounded particles.
Rounded grains	●	Rounded particles; the result of rounding by vapor transfer or partial melting.
Faceted crystals	□	Angular grains with facets on some surfaces. The early stage of the recrystallization process.
Depth hoar	∧	Partially or fully developed cups; lines and layering on crystal faces are recognizable. Advanced stage of the recrystallization process.
Melt-freeze particles	○	Irregular, rounded grain clusters after melting and refreezing; voids between individual crystals are filled with water.
Surface hoar	V	Feather-like or shallow cup-like crystals with lines on the crystal faces; result of deposition of water vapor from the atmosphere.

Fig. 5.21 Using a magnifying glass to look at depth hoar crystals.

Fig. 5.22 This thin section cut out of the wall of the snowpit and viewed against the light shows a 13 cm layer of partially settled snow between harder isothermal layers. When the snow is firm enough, this is an instructive way to view the layering. Photo by Bruce Jamieson.

5. Using the crystal screen, determine the size of the grains in each layer by comparing the largest dimension with the line spacing on the crystal screen. Disregard the small particles. Record the size or range of sizes to the nearest 0.1 mm in column 4 (D for Diameter). If you have no means of measuring the grains estimate the size and record as follows:

Grain Size	
Class	Size
Very fine	0 - 0.5 mm
Fine	0.5 - 1.0 mm
Medium	1.0 - 2.0 mm
Coarse	2.0 - 4.0 mm
Very coarse	4.0 mm or more

6. Pick up a handful of snow and squeeze it in a gloved hand. Record the free water content in column 5 (W for Water content).

Liquid Water Content		
Class	%	Description
Dry	0%	The snow crumbles when crushed, the grains having little tendency to stick together.
Moist	< 3%	The snow sticks together and a snowball forms. Water is not visible, even with the aid of a magnifying glass.
Wet	3 - 8 %	Water can be recognized between adjacent snow grains, but water cannot be pressed out.
Very wet	8 - 15%	Water can be pressed out by moderately squeezing snow in the hand.
Slush	> 15%	The snow is flooded; water runs out when a sample is picked up.

7. Make a shovel shear test, a loaded column test, and a Rutschblock test on the walls of the snow pit. Record the results as comments in your notebook.

8. Make an assessment of snow stability based on your observations. Record your assessment at the bottom of the page.

9. Fill in the pit if it's likely to be a danger to other people.

Snowcraft cannot be learned in the classroom nor can it be learned by reading about it in a book. It can only be learned out there in the mountains after many hours of experiencing different snow conditions at different times of the year. Each time you go out make a determined effort to think about what is happening in the snowpack beneath your feet. Experienced travellers subconsciously note a myriad of small facts and occurrences which are tucked away in their memory to be recalled and used as necessary.

Fig. 5.23 Make at least one shovel test on the walls of the snow pit to identify potential sliding layers. Photo by Bob Sandford, courtesy Alberta Mountain Council.

Fig. 6.1 Many skiers and climbers fail to recognize dangerous avalanche terrain. When instability is extreme, slopes like this one, above the normal route to Dolomite Pass in the Canadian Rockies, can be triggered from below and enough snow released to bury a person in the valley bottom.

6

Recognizing Avalanche Terrain

Recognition of avalanche terrain, the most important factor in avalanche safety, allows the skier and climber to either avoid potentially dangerous areas completely or if this isn't possible, to pick a route which reduces the risk to the minimum. Avalanche terrain is defined as any area steep enough to slide or any area close enough to steep slopes to become part of the track or deposition zone of an avalanche. As you try to identify potential avalanche slopes remember that avalanches usually occur where they have always run in the past. Be alert for any signs of previous activity. Also, consider where the debris from an avalanche will end up. Will it be spread out over an easy angled open slope or piled deep in the bottom of a ravine? How deep could you be buried?

Slope Angle

The basic terrain feature necessary for avalanching is a steep slope. How steep and how can you judge the steepness? Studies of slab avalanches have shown that the majority originate on slopes between 30° and 45°, although the critical angle for slab avalanches can range from as little as 25° to 55° or greater. Wet snow avalanches have been reported on slopes as shallow as 15°. On such a shallow slope wet snow avalanches move very slowly, though they may move long distances and are unlikely to be dangerous to the traveller providing no other hazards such as cliff bands are present. Loose snow slides on slopes in the same angle range as slab avalanches. The angle of repose is dependent upon the type of snow crystal; it's low for wet slushy snow becoming higher as the snow becomes grainier and well sintered. Usually loose dry snow sluffs harmlessly off steeper slopes during or shortly after a storm. In the highest mountains and in Coastal Alpine zones such as the Cascades and the Scottish Highlands snow can be plastered on very steep faces with slab forming on slopes of up to 60°.

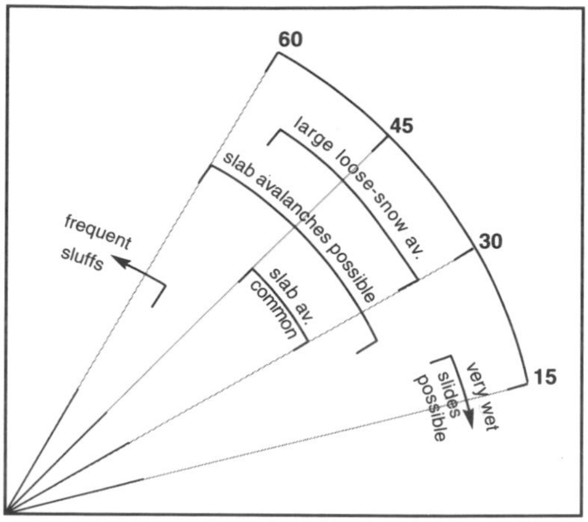

Fig. 6.2 Most frequent slope angles for avalanches.

30° An enjoyable, challenging slope for the good downhill skier and the expert cross-country downhiller. Cross-country skiers will probably be kick turning and traversing. The average talus slope in the mountains is about 30 degrees.

40° An expert downhill skier will feel exhilarated on such a slope. Anyone less than expert will feel decidedly uncomfortable. Few cross-country skiers, even expert cross-country downhillers, would venture on a slope of such steepness.

How to Judge Slope Angle

Judging slope angle is not easy. Fortunately, most of us tend to overestimate it and so keep off the steeper slopes. The most accurate way is to use an inclinometer. Life-Link make a simple, inexpensive plastic model and a number of compasses now on the market such as the Silva 15TDCL Ranger and the Wilkie M110PN have simple clinometers built into them. Here's a quick, simple guide for skiers to use:

20° Intermediate downhill terrain. Competent cross-country skiers will be able to parallel ski in good conditions.

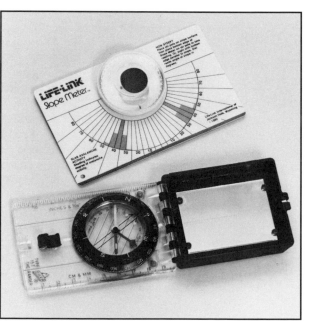

Fig. 6.3 Clinometers are built into some compasses or may be made especially for avalanche hazard evaluation.

Terrain Features

The mountainside is made up of bowls, terraces, gullies, steep uniform slopes, convex and concave slopes, ridges, cliffs and so on. Some of these features provide routes safe from avalanches; others are death traps. The term **terrain traps** is used to describe small, often innocuous looking terrain features which can trap the unwary traveller.

Steep, Straight Slopes

These are obviously potential avalanche slopes. On long open slopes it's difficult to predict where the starting zone for avalanches may be, though often avalanches start at some discontinuity in the slope such as exposed rock outcrops.

Convex Slopes

Many avalanches start where there is some change in slope profile. The rounded top to a peak or ridge can be the trigger zone for slab avalanches. This is because creep due to weight of snow down the steeper part of the slope sets up tensile stresses in the snowpack which are greatest in the rounded portion of the slope above. Any small disturbance is sufficient to relieve these stresses by the cracking of the snowpack and subsequent avalanche.

In some cases the crown line of avalanches on open convex slopes occurs at the point where the convex slope becomes straight, indicating that the convex portion of the slope influences the formation of slab rather than setting up stresses leading to failure. The main danger of convex slopes is that they lead the traveller onto slopes of increasing steepness with a corresponding increase in the probability of avalanche release.

Concave Slopes

Concave slopes are generally considered to be safer than convex slopes, but this is not always the case; a lee concave slope, with possibly a cornice at the top, can be just as deadly. There are several recorded incidents where a party, traversing on the safe-looking flat bottom part of the slope, triggered a slab avalanche and were buried by the mass of snow descending from above.

In the absence of soft slab, the snow at the bottom will tend to support the snowpack higher up. But if the lower layer of the snowpack is depth hoar there is a danger that any undercutting, by a ski track or by wind erosion for example, will bring the whole slope down (see Fig. 10.3 page 165).

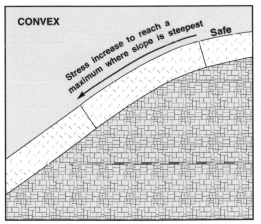

Fig. 6.4 The most likely fracture point is where stresses are maximum. Terrain breaks such as cliff bands or rocks may also create lines of weakness.

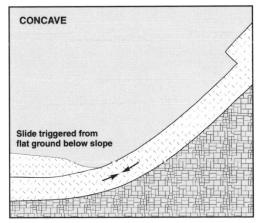

Fig. 6.5 When instability is high, snow on concave slopes can be triggered from flat ground below.

Terraces

Terraces tend to prevent avalanching until later in the season when sufficient snow covers them over to form a continuous slope. Although early season slides tend to end up part way down the avalanche path, retained on the terraced sections, these deposition areas can easily bury a fallen skier, so treat terraces with caution.

Bowls

Bowls with rounded concave sides and straight slopes leading into them are among the most dangerous terrain traps. Their shape makes them susceptible to the deposition of slab and in addition they often have narrow restricted outlets which allow the snow to funnel down and pile up many metres deep at the bottom. Unfortunately, such bowls offer tempting skiing

Fig. 6.6 Benches across an avalanche path allow enough snow to accumulate to bury a person. See also the comment about ten platforms on page 20.

Fig. 6.7 Bowls, like the one to the left of the photograph, are among the most dangerous terrain features. Evaluate snow conditions very carefully before you take off down any steep bowl. Stick to ridges where possible. Photo by Clair Israelson.

118

Fig. 6.8 Green Gully, Ben Nevis, Scotland. Photo by Hamish MacInnes.

Many fatal accidents to winter climbers occur in gullies, probably because they present the easiest way up or down the mountain. Scotland, which is renowned for its fine gully climbs (the term gully being rather loosely defined sometimes —the bottom section of Zero Gully is a 400 foot vertical corner bulging with overhangs), has, in recent winters, seen an alarming increase in the number of avalanche accidents. In the winter of 1982 four separate avalanche accidents killed three people within an hour or two of each other on the Ben Nevis massif. Three of the accidents occurred in gullies. The day was sunny and calm, hardly a harbinger of tragedy, but prior to that the weather had been stormy; falls of heavy snow accumulating on a thawed and refrozen old snow surface had created ideal avalanche conditions. In the first accident, a tier of snow sliding from a terrace on the buttress above swept a party of five climbers almost 200 metres to the bottom of Castle Gully. The uninjured climbers dug out their companions but by that time only one was alive. Half an hour later, a 19 year old girl standing at the foot of Gardyloo Gully died from an avalanche presumably triggered by her two companions above. One survivor was uninjured; the other broke his femur when the rope, which had wound round his legs, snagged on a boulder and came to a sudden stop. Not long after this, two climbers were swept down No. 2 Gully and another group triggered a slab avalanche while descending the Carn Mor Dearg Arete. Somehow, both parties escaped with only minor injuries.

The growing sport of waterfall ice climbing has been luring climbers into gullies which were formerly avoided. If you are contemplating an ice climb in a steep gully with a collection zone above, you should wait until you are sure the snow above has either fallen or has become stabilized.

Gullies

Steep gullies form natural deposition zones for slab and natural chutes for loose falling snow. Avalanche starting zones are difficult to pinpoint; there may be many different side branches higher up the main gully which can't be seen from down below. Collection zones above are often large and again, it's difficult to predict from below if and how they become loaded with snow. There is usually little warning of the avalanche coming and often there is no escape. Keep away from shallow gullies on open slopes; the slight depression they make in the slope is an ideal location for slab to form.

Ridges

Wide gently-angled ridges offer the safest route of travel. Narrower ridges, although probably still the best route to a summit, can pose the problem of cornices; a problem compounded by bad visibility. Very often, because of the action of wind across the top of such a ridge, the windward side will give good firm footing, whereas the opposite side, below the cornice, will be smothered in deep soft snow in precarious condition. If the ridge is corniced on both sides you've got problems.

Cirques

Amphitheaters ringed by peaks or ridges can be the scene of extensive slab avalanching, the fracture line travelling rapidly round the whole cirque and releasing large volumes of snow making escape virtually impossible. One example of this is the cirque below Mount Sir Donald and Uto Peak in the Selkirk Range of British Columbia; in heavy snowfall years, the cirque produces a large climax avalanche which fills the valley at the foot of the Illecillewaet Glacier with some 10 to 15 metres of snow.

Canyons and Gorges

These features are natural depositories for avalanching snow. You should ask yourself, what kind of slopes feed in from above? How much snow is on them and is it stable? Even a very small slide can pile up enough snow in the bottom of a canyon to bury a person. This happened to a skier in Leeks Canyon, Wyoming. His presence on a 45 side slope above the canyon caused a small slab to fail and down he went to the bottom, buried up to his waist. He probably would have escaped unscathed if the first slide hadn't triggered a second slide which in turn triggered a third. He was found two days later under 3 metres of debris. It's sobering to realize that the slides ran less than 60 metres and the combined width of all three was less than 100 metres.

Fig. 6.9 Photo taken during the search for the buried skier in Leeks Canyon, Wyoming/ Photo courtesy Dale Gallagher, U.S. Forest Service.

Flat Ground

When travelling or setting up camp it's important to consider the shape and length of runout zones in the event of an avalanche occurring. The outrun from large avalanches can travel many kilometres across flat ground; in a restricted valley avalanches can flow up the opposite slope removing trees and depositing debris on the way.

Keep well away from the foot of steep slopes when hazard is high; there have been a number of cases of parties on seemingly safe slopes triggering the steeper slopes above. This happened to a group of four skiers in February 1979. They had followed the summer trail into the basin at the foot of Stanley Glacier in Kootenay National Park, passing a sign warning of avalanche danger on the way. After stopping for lunch on the flat valley bottom, they climbed an easy angled talus slope on the north side of the basin, making several switchbacks. A few moments after they started to ski down, a large slab, — 450 metres long and 300 metres wide — released from a chute high above them, and carried them 300 metres down the valley. Another party in the vicinity quickly dug out the two partially buried skiers and found a third person within half an hour but failed to revive him after two and a half hours of effort. Because of extreme avalanche danger caused by further snowfall and the lack of any escape route for the rescuers in the event of a further slide, the search for the fourth person, a girl, was delayed until the surrounding slopes had been bombed from a helicopter. She was found 2 days later under 4 metres of snow.

Fig. 6.10 The route to Bow hut in the Canadian Rockies leads up this narrow canyon. Fortunately, the slopes above this canyon rarely avalanche.

121

Terrain Traps

Fig. 6.11 Note the old fracture line on this steep side slope above the V-shaped valley below.

Fig. 6.13 This slab avalanche on the Zermatt Breithorn carried the skier across the bridged crevasse. Had the crevasse been open at this point she would have been swept in and buried under may metres of snow. Photo by Al Schaffer.

Fig. 6.12 This short 30° slope occasionally releases enough snow to pile up 2 metres deep against the rock and trees.

ig. 6.14 Consider what is below the slope you are crossing. sk yourself: where will I end up if it does slide.

Fig. 6.15 In this case, you would probably end up at the bottom of the cliff.

Surface Roughness

The surface of the ground has a major influence on early season avalanching. Roughness of surface determines the snow depth needed to fill irregularities, controls the amount of creep and significantly affects the ability of the snow to avalanche to the ground in many regions.

Generally, the rougher the ground surface the more snow depth is required before avalanching will take place; broken terrain and boulder fields won't become avalanche slopes until sufficient snow has fallen to cover most of the rocks. On the other hand, smooth grass slopes, talus slopes and smooth rock slabs need little snow before avalanching occurs and will avalanche to bare ground frequently throughout the winter.

Professional hazard evaluators are using a figure of 30 to 60 cm, depending on location, as the minimum snow depth necessary to cover roughness of ground before natural avalanching occurs. This figure applies to many areas but should not be taken as an infallible rule of thumb. For instance, in the Canadian Rockies during the early winter of 1981-82, little snow and cold temperatures resulted in a snowpack that was almost entirely composed of recrystallized grains (depth hoar and faceted crystals); in many locations the snow had enough internal cohesion to enable it to form potential slab avalanches. Because rocks were showing through the snow many skiers thought the slopes were safe to cross. The avalanches they released flowed round the rocks like granulated sugar; even slopes with as little as 15 cm of snow were avalanching right down to the ground. There were many lucky escapes.

Fig. 6.16 A wet-snow avalanche which slid on the smooth rocks of the Great Slab, Coire an Lochain, Scotland. Photo by Rod Ward.

Fig. 6.17 A down-to-the ground slab avalanche on smooth grass. Davos. Photo by André Roch.

Effect of Vegetation

Another factor which influences avalanching is ground cover and vegetation. Grass provides an ideal sliding surface for snow. Willows and slide alder tend to stabilize snow early in the season, but later on, due to creep of the snow cover, are bent over until they are lying parallel to the ground, thus becoming a much less effective barrier. In cold dry climates, the air spaces provided by brushy ground cover like willows and alder allow the development of large depth hoar crystals which provide a weak layer at the bottom of the snowpack.

Light timber, defined as timber which you can ski through without too much difficulty, is no protection; slabs can form from wind eddies. Unless you have detailed local knowledge, pinpointing actual avalanche locations is very difficult. Heavy timber, that is virtually impossible to ski through, is usually safe although abnormally large avalanches may break through from above.

Four skiers were killed in a massive avalanche in the Canadian Rockies during a major avalanche cycle during which 85 cm of snow had fallen in the past 24 hours. Skiing a popular ski trail, they had crossed the path near the very bottom, and had probably stopped to get something out of their packs about 20 m into the heavy timber on the far side. A cornice break 350 m above the skiers triggered the huge snow-laden bowl. The airborne avalanche blasted into the timber, severing mature trees and stripping branches 10 m up the trunks of those left standing.

Deforestation and reforestation play a large part in avalanche development and control. Areas recently deforested may show no sign of previous avalanche activity which doesn't mean they are safe to ski. Treat such areas with caution, assessing snow conditions as you would for any other open slope.

Fig. 6.18 Lightly-timbered slopes such as this one are no protection against soft slab avalanches.

Fig. 6.19 A careful assessment of snow stability is necessary before descending cornice-hung lee slopes. This ski touring party in St. Mary's Alpine Park, British Columbia took off their skis and walked down using the rock buttress on the right for protection.
Photo Al Schaffer.

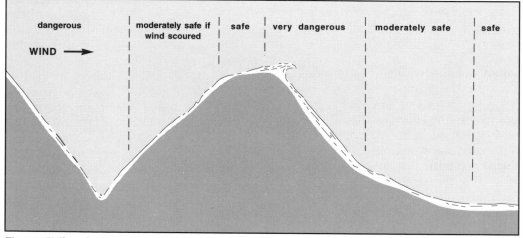

Fig. 6.20 V-Shaped valley bottoms and lee slopes are the most dangerous routes to travel. Ridge tops and flat ground well way from the foot of steep slopes are the safest.

126

Slope Orientation

A slope's orientation to sun and wind is very important. When considering their effect on north and south slopes and on lee and windward slopes, don't forget that slopes with other aspects will exhibit characteristics somewhere between the two extremes and that a heavy, uniform, windless fall of snow may make windward slopes just as avalanche prone as lee slopes. In certain conditions of wind, temperature and humidity, soft slab can form over an entire mountainside.

Orientation to the Sun

Heat gain and loss from a snow surface is dependent on the angle of the slope, the direction it faces, it's latitude and the season. In midwinter, when the sun is low in the sky, south-facing slopes receive sun almost at right angles to the surface thereby obtaining the maximum possible radiation. During the same period, north-facing slopes receive almost no radiation. As an example of the way latitude affects avalanche characteristics consider the Canadian Rockies and southern Colorado Rockies. Although these two areas have a similar snowfall with cold temperatures and clear nights enhancing the formation of depth hoar, the difference in latitude between Colorado which is 39° and the Canadian Rockies which is 52° results in much greater radiation on south slopes during the day in Colorado and the subsequent formation of layers of recrystallized snow. This tends to build up layers of firm well settled snow separated by thin layers of weak crystalline snow which are potential sliding layers. The usual concept of south slopes stabilizing under the effect of increased radiation cannot be applied in southern latitudes.

South Slopes Because south-facing slopes receive the most solar radiation, rounding proceeds more rapidly than on other slopes; stabilization and settlement is faster. Although south-facing slopes, not taking into account other factors such as wind direction and terrain features, tend to be the safest during mid winter, they're often indicator slopes; that is, they are the first to release avalanches during and shortly after a storm. If there's enough radiation available for melting, sun crusting will occur. As spring approaches and the days get warmer melting results in snowballs or wet snow avalanches. Previously safe slopes now become dangerous.

North slopes North slopes receive little or no sunlight in midwinter and, therefore, are subject to maximum cooling by outgoing long wave radiation. Because the snow tends to be cooler and rounding slow, avalanche danger extends for longer periods after a storm. Lower temperatures also provide the optimum conditions for the formation of depth hoar which is likely to persist as a weak layer in the snow cover for a greater part of the season. By spring, conditions are reversed; north slopes may provide a route safe from wet snow avalanches when south-facing slopes are dangerous.

Orientation to Wind

Lee slopes Lee slopes can be very dangerous: they are subject to a rapid accumulation of snow during a storm or during fine, but windy weather. Such slopes are often overhung by cornices which can break off and trigger an avalanche on the slope below. It's important to remember that the aspect of a lee slope can vary around a mountainside depending on local air currents. To complicate matters further, both lee and windward slopes can form on the same side of a mountain. Individual ridges, stands of trees or outcrops of rock will also have their own localized lee slopes. The majority of avalanche accident involving backcountry skiers take place on lee slopes.

Windward Slopes Slopes exposed to wind tend to receive less snow deposition. The resulting shallow snowpack may result in the formation of depth hoar, but usually, the snow is more firmly compacted by wind action. Rime deposits on windward slopes give an indication of wind direction as do formations such as sastrugi and etched layers.

Determining Wind Direction

Lacking specific meteorological data, wind direction is best evaluated by observing natural features which are either the result of erosion or of deposition. As a general rule, eroded features such as sastrugi have their steep sides and sharp edges on the windward side whereas deposited features, such as snow drifts, have smoother, more rounded shapes facing the wind. The most useful features to look for are as follows:

Cornices

Cornices are deposits of wind-drifted snow overhanging the lee side of a ridge or other terrain with suitable configuration. Although they're reliable indicators of past wind direction, they don't necessarily indicate the direction of the wind at the present time. It may be argued that cornices form even if the wind doesn't strike the ridge at right angles. This may be so, but snow is still deposited on the lee side, and that is all you are worried about.

Double cornices which overhang both sides of a ridge and cornices which alternate from one side of a ridge to the other are formed by unusually turbulent and distorted wind patterns which make any kind of prediction of wind direction fruitless.

Blowing snow

During windy weather you can look up at the mountains and see plumes of snow streaming off the ridge tops. The length of the plume gives you the wind speed — moderate or strong is good enough for your purpose — and the amount of snow indicates how fast deposition is taking place on the lee slopes.

Fig. 6.21 Cornices are good indicators of past wind direction. This mature cornice on the summit of Mount Temple, Canadian Rockies, shows the direction of the prevailing wind. Photo by Gillean Daffern.

Fig. 6.22 Snow blowing off the top of Mount Lefroy, Canadian Rockies indicates present wind direction at that altitude. Photo by Lars Suneby.

Drifting

Drifts around trees and rocks are a sure indication of wind direction. The smooth rounded end of a drift faces into the wind; the long tail tapers away on the lee side. In winds of moderate speed, eddies form vertically and scour out wind scoops around the base of obstacles such as trees, rocks and even whole buildings.

Sastrugi

Sastrugi or Skalvar is the term used to describe the large scale erosion of a snow surface into a series of waves and projections. They're usually associated with strong, continuous winds blowing over long periods; in the Polar regions they reach a height of a metre or more. More modest formations are found in the North American mountains, but even so, skiing through sastrugi is a wretched tip-breaking business. Sometimes the wind removes enough of the surface snow to reach softer layers underneath and then the projection becomes undercut. The steep faces are always on the windward side.

Rime

Rime, a reliable indicator of wind direction, can be observed on any prominent object standing above the snow surface such as rocks or trees. Rime deposits always grow into the wind; the heavier the deposit and the longer the branches, the higher the wind speed. The presence of rime also indicates that snow on the windward slopes has been strengthened, even cemented in place, by deposits of rime.

Vegetation

In alpine areas near treeline, vegetation is a good indicator of prevailing wind direction. Trees may lean away from the wind or have significantly less growth on the windward side. Small trees leaning down slope are probably doing so from creep of the snowpack or from past avalanche activity.

Fig. 6.24 Small trees which lean down-slope are the result of snow creep and regular avalanche activity. See also Fig. 5.3 page 94.

Fig. 6.23 Small sastrugi showing etching and some undercutting. Photo by Chris Stethem.

129

Recognizing Avalanche Slopes

Most major avalanche slopes can be easily recognized: clean swaths cut through the forest, steep treeless gullies and steep open slopes are obvious. Few people get caught on the obvious slopes. Usually its the relatively small insignificant slopes which are the killers; no-one has noticed the subtle changes of terrain features onto which they have unthinkingly strayed. While there is no substitute for local experience in such areas, there are often indistinct signs which can be picked up by careful observation.

Look for signs of previous avalanche activity: trees with lower branches missing or broken, decapitated trees, trees with no limbs or fresh scars on the uphill side. In open skiable timber they may be your only indication. Look out for fracture lines where a slope has cracked but not avalanched, a change in snow depth and texture, mounds of snow or dirty snow mixed with rocks and upturned trees. During summer travel notice the location of avalanche debris and of lingering snow patches in gullies and valley bottoms.

Fig. 6.25 Some terrain features like this gully with a large collection zone above are easily recognized as avalanche terrain.

Fig. 6.26 Missing branches and scars on the uphill side of trees are signs of avalanche activity.

7

Hazard Evaluation

Avalanche hazard evaluation is the process of deciding whether or not you are in danger from potential avalanches. **Hazard forecasting** is an attempt to predict if that danger is increasing or decreasing. Both hazard evaluation and hazard forecasting utilize information gathered about the type of terrain, past and present weather conditions and the state of the snowpack. By sifting the many items of information you should be able to isolate those factors which are relevant to your present situation. Remember that in each geographical snow area certain items of information will be more important than others and that these can vary as the season progresses.

Certain indications of danger are relevant to all areas and should not be ignored:

— Evidence of avalanche activity on slopes of similar orientation.

— Settling and fracturing of the snow cover.

— New snow accompanied by high winds.

— A sudden warming trend.

Fig. 7.1 Skiers and climbers are becoming aware of the need to evaluate avalanche hazard. Signs like this one are no substitution for specific warning programs. Photo by Clair Israelson.

Local Knowledge

Ideally, hazard evaluation starts with local knowledge of an area gained by summer hiking plus several winter seasons of travel. A person armed with such knowledge has a tremendous advantage over the skier with no local experience. Unfortunately, there's no easy way of obtaining the information: most trail guides only note the more obvious hazards and word-of-mouth information is notoriously unreliable.

Seasons History

Each time you go out you add to your knowledge of the seasons snowpack. How much fresh snow has fallen since your last trip? Has it consolidated? Does a layer of depth hoar still exist on certain slopes? Have any paths avalanched since your last visit? You should speculate why conditions have changed or why a slope has avalanched.

Ed LaChapelle sums it up when he says; *"The person who wonders about snow stability only when standing on the edge of an avalanche path about to be crossed has thought of the problem too late."* He also says that you *"should always have an opinion, no matter how vague or inaccurate, about the current state of snow stability"*.

With experience you will be able to revise and refine it to arrive at a more accurate evaluation.

Don't limit your observations to your ski trip; you can see a lot from your car window just travelling to the area. News items in local papers or radio stations about roads blocked by avalanches, accidents or ski area closures all help to build up an overall picture as the winter progresses. You've seen those pre-season stickers for downhill skiers "Think Snow". Thinking snow all season will make your trip into the backcountry not only more enjoyable but a lot safer.

Regional Characteristics of Snow

Anyone who has skied extensively in North America and Europe will realize that snow conditions vary considerably from region to region. Andre Roch — Swiss mountaineer and avalanche consultant — classified the western USA, and by that token western Canada, into three major areas of alpine climate: the Eastern Alpine Zone, the Middle Alpine Zone and the Coastal Alpine Zone. Each has a different type of snowfall, a different form of avalanche hazard and requires a different approach to hazard evaluation. Generally, most mountain ranges in the world contain zones with similar characteristics to these three categories.

The boundaries of these zones are not always well defined; overlaps and inconsistencies occur and sometimes characteristics of two different zones can be found in one area in the same season. For example, conditions more normally found in the Coastal Alpine Zone such as rain or snowfall with very high humidity sometimes occur at Whitefish downhill ski area in Montana some 1000 km inland and Alta ski area in Utah exhibits characteristics of both the Eastern and Middle Alpine Zones depending on the season.

Try to relate the conditions found in each zone to your own home area.

Eastern Alpine Zone

The Eastern Alpine Zone, such as the Canadian Rockies and the Colorado Rockies, tends to receive moderate snowfalls at fairly low rates of precipitation. Few storms deposit more than 30 cm of new snow. One to 2 cm per hour is the more normal maximum, the new snow often falling at temperatures below -20°C and accompanied by strong winds which cause extensive drifting. Cold temperatures and low humidity result in a dry powdery snow and a tendency for the snowpack to be shallow and unstable. Depth hoar is common. Midwinter rain or melting is rare. **The principle hazard comes from slab avalanches of the delayed-action type** which often involves the whole snowpack right down to the ground.

Early winter has the least predictable snow conditions; the snowpack is often shallow and uncompacted leading to recrystallization. Without doubt its the most dangerous time of the year to be travelling in the mountains. In this zone climbers should be especially careful. The accident on Chancellor Peak in early December 1976, which killed Leif Patterson and two companions, is directly attributable to treacherous early-season conditions: drifting snow had formed a hard slab over depth hoar in the gully they were climbing. It's surmised that because the snow appeared hard, the climbers believed conditions were similar to those of an early morning in summer.

Professional forecasting is usually based on examination of the snow structure plus evaluation of meteorological conditions, especially wind and new snowfall. You should ask about earlier periods of prolonged cold — an indication of the amount of depth hoar — and look for signs of wind having caused significant drifting. Recent snowfalls of 15 cm or more may be ready to slide on surface hoar or depth hoar layers. Using a ski pole, test all the way down to the ground for weak layers. Because slab formation is often localized, test frequently. Check for sliding layers using the Shovel Shear test and repeat whenever the terrain you are travelling across changes in aspect. If you suspect hard slab keep off the steeper slopes. Suspect all lee slopes, especially minor ones such as the sheltered side of slight hollows, ridges or gullies. Look for signs of wind direction by observing minor drifts, cornices or other wind formations. Test skiing is not a reliable indication of stability. **Keen observation, good routefinding and extreme caution are the keys to safe travel.**

By mid season, during the months of February and March, avalanche activity is usually, but not always, more predictable. Obviously the further north you are the less predictable the mid-season avalanching will be because winters are colder and last longer at higher latitudes. Now that the snowpack has built-up, the major hazard comes from new-snow avalanches sliding on the old snow surface. Observing your tracks on switchbacks and using the Shovel Shear and Rutschblock tests will give an indication of how deep that sliding layer is and how easily it slides.

When temperatures start to warm up in spring, wet snow avalanches are the norm. The snowpack must be examined to determine the depth of the wet layer. Spring ski tourers should keep off steep south and west-facing slopes in the afternoon. Conversely, north and east-facing slopes, which were the most dangerous early in the season, now offer the safest route if the temperature of the snowpack is several degrees below freezing.

Middle Alpine Zone

The Middle Alpine Zone, for example Rogers Pass in the Selkirk Range of British Columbia, is characterized by heavy snowfalls which can deposit a metre or more of new snow per storm. The snow, which varies from dry to moist, falls at a high rate of 3 to 5 cm per hour and comes with medium strong winds, medium temperatures and often a high relative humidity. Midwinter rain or melting is rare. This zone is notorious for the fast loading of its slopes by fresh snowfall often accompanied by wind, which in conjunction with the high humidity common to this area leads to the formation of extensive areas of soft slab. **The principal hazard is from large, direct-action soft-slab avalanches.** Depth hoar is rare but when it does occur can lead to full depth climax avalanches.

Find out the details of any snowfall within the past week. A rate of 2 cm or more an hour is a hazard indicator. Ask about any unusual weather conditions before the last storm such as very cold spells, recent rain or thaws and clear cold nights which encourage the formation of surface hoar: all these indicate a potential sliding layer within the snowpack. Wait two or three days after a major snowstorm before venturing onto or crossing under steep slopes. Ski pole tests will indicate the depth of the new snow, but in this area will likely miss layering within the snowpack so it's as well to test right down to the well-settled snow. Repeat the test on each new slope or new exposure and at every 200 m change in altitude. Sliding layers may be deep, so use test skiing cautiously. Suspect all lee and partial lee slopes but remember that in the Middle Alpine Zone extensive soft slab can form over the entire area without regard to wind.

Spring conditions are basically the same. The only difference is that the generally higher temperatures promote a faster settlement and bonding of new snow to the old snowpack. At the same time, changes within the snowpack leading to dangerous conditions are accelerated; rain will warm up the entire snowpack very quickly and then you get an extensive cycle of wet-snow avalanching.

Coastal Alpine Zone

The Coastal Alpine Zone is typical of most maritime mountain areas such as the Coast Ranges of Alaska, Washington and British Columbia and the mountains of Scotland. This zone has snowfalls of damp to wet snow deposited at moderate temperatures and often at a high rate. Because midwinter rain and surface melting is common, settlement of the snow cover tends to be rapid leading to basically stable conditions. Around and above timberline high storm winds form extensive rime deposits on rocks and trees — a good indicator of wind direction. **The principal hazard is from direct action damp and wet soft-slab avalanches.** Although wind may play a part in avalanche formation, especially on very steep faces which have been plastered with snow from strong driving winds, the biggest factors in this area are the rate of snowfall, the depth of the newly fallen snow, rapid temperature rises, rain and dense or icy layers in the old snowpack.

Find out the dates, amounts and duration of snowfalls and rainfalls within the past week. Ask about extended periods of fine weather with clear nights prior to storms which enhance the quick formation of surface recrystallized grains known colloquially on the west coast of Canada as "West Coast Depth Hoar!". Learn what the recent range of temperature has been; specifically, you want to know whether the temperature has been above freezing, whether it stayed above freezing overnight and whether it increased during a snowstorm in the past few days. Look for buried crusts which could form sliding surfaces for the snow above.

Test down to the well-settled old snow, using the handle end of the ski pole if necessary. Use the Shovel Shear test to check for sliding layers. Check the snowpack carefully for the presence of free water especially if you notice water appearing on large rounded ice grains overlying any impermeable layer. Hazard from wet-snow avalanching can develop extremely quickly in this zone, so try and plan your route for the cooler slopes.

Wait two days after a major storm before trusting any steep slopes. The worst avalanche conditions often occur when a crusted or settled old snow surface is covered with an initial deposit of cold feathery snow with little wind. If the temperature rises and the wind picks up during the progression of the storm, heavier denser snow will fall on top of the loose layer which in turn is lying above a good sliding layer to which it is poorly bonded.

Rapid thaws are particularly dangerous; firm stable snow can turn into slush within an hour. Both the increase in altitude and the chilling effect of strong wind make it difficult to detect a change in temperature as you climb higher up the mountain. In January 1970 four climbers set out to climb the Italian Route on Ben Nevis. Because the climb was in such good condition, they reached the final relatively easy snow slopes leading to Tower Ridge early in the day and decided to extend their route by taking a more diagonal line which was largely unexplored. High winds had deposited a tremendous amount of snow on the lee side of the ridge.

The survivor recounted, *"During this period there was a very remarkable rise in temperature which wasn't apparent to us at the time. The wind was very high — a tremendous wind — and the cooling effect of this wind belied the temperature rise"*. (Rescuers later found the snow lower down dripping with water.) As they were crossing a large basin, the snow fractured to a depth of over one metre and carried three of the climbers down to their deaths some 300 metres below. The fourth member of the group had, at the critical moment, untied the rope to flick it free of a snag and was left stranded on the climb.

Fig. 7.2 Snow-plastered Crowberry Gully in Glencoe, Scotland, is typical of winter conditions in Coastal Alpine Zones, Sudden thaws lead to extreme avalanche hazard. Photo by Hamish MacInnes.

Hazard Evaluation

Assume that you're standing on the edge of a large, open slope with an undetermined depth of snow. You don't have to cross this slope, but the only reasonable alternative is to turn back. You have taken all the recommended precautions and are aware of past weather conditions. How do you go about evaluating this slope? Ask yourself 4 questions:

— Could the slope produce avalanches?

— Could the snow fail?

— What will happen to me if the slope avalanches?

— Will conditions get worse?

1. Could the slope produce avalanches?

Is the slope steep enough to slide? If it isn't, then ask **Are there dangerous slopes above**? If the answer is no to both questions, then you have no worries. But don't forget that wet snow can slide down less steep slopes than dry-slab avalanches. Judge steepness by asking yourself, **"Would I ski straight down it or not"**. Relate the answer to your skiing ability.

Critical   — *Slopes greater than 30°.*
           — *Variations in incline*
           — *cliff bands.*

What's the orientation of the slope to wind? Look for signs of wind direction such as cornices, drifts around trees and rocks, rime etc. Consider the aspect of the slope.

What's the orientation of the slope to sun? If temperatures are above freezing and the snow is showing signs of melting consider the orientation of the slope. Think about your route later in the day.

Critical   — *South and south-west slopes exposed to strong radiation*
           — *First major thaw of spring*

What's the nature of the slope? How wide is the slope? How long will you be exposed to danger if you do decide to cross. Are there signs of the slope avalanching previously such as channels in the snow or debris at the bottom. Examine the collection zone above the slope. Is there a lot of fresh snow up there? Does it have the smooth rounded appearance of slab?

Critical   — *open slopes*
           — *thin forest*
           — *confined slide path*
           — *gully or bowl*

2. Is the snow stable? Could it fail?

How deep is the snowpack? In some areas a minimum depth of snow is required before avalanches can develop. The normally accepted figures are 30 cm for smooth ground and 60 cm for rough ground. In the Eastern Alpine Zone, however, this general rule doesn't apply. If the base has been weakened by depth hoar, avalanches can occur with as little as 12 cm to 15 cm of snow; the loose "sugar snow" crystals flow around rocks and trees which in other zones would hold the snow in place.

Are there any signs of avalanche activity? Be constantly on the lookout for any signs of instability. Why is snow sluffing off steep cliffs, or snowballs rolling down a sunlit slope? Note any slab avalanches, old or new, and consider why they have formed. Are similar slopes still unstable? What about slopes of other aspects? Might they be dangerous too?

What layers are there in the snowpack? Have you investigated the layering of the snowpack by digging a snowpit, doing a shovel test and a Rutschblock test ? Do you need to?

Critical   — *very hard or unusually soft layers*
           — *weak bond between layers*
           — *20 cm or more of snow above a weak layer*
           — *loose, cold snow (faceted grains)*
           — *wet snow*

Fig. 7.3 Be constantly on the lookout for any sign of instability such as the small sluff in the centre right of the photograph. Photo by Al Schaffer.

How much fresh snow has fallen? Most avalanches fall during or shortly after storms, so any appreciable snowfall is an indication of potential avalanche hazard. Heavy damp snow, in particular, loads a slope very rapidly to the point of failure. The rate of precipitation in terms of mm/hr of water content is a better indicator of loading than actual snow depth; a dry cold snowfall may contain little precipitation. When hazard is already extreme a light snowfall may be all that is required to trigger extensive avalanching. The amount of settlement is important and any settlement less than 15% per day of the storm snow should be viewed with suspicion.

Critical   — *snowfall greater than*
  2 cm per hour
— *new snow depth greater*
  than 30 cm
— *slow settlement of new snow*
— *very light or very heavy snow*
— *heavily rimed crystals,*
  graupel
— *heavy stiff layer above a*
  light weak layer
— *rain*
— *easy shovel test on new snow*
  layer or Rutschblock fails
  when stepped on

Wind Light winds tend to toughen up the surface of the snowpack by forming wind crust which gives unpleasant skiing conditions for a day or two. If the wind is warm and dry there is little effect on the snowpack apart from a speeding up of evaporation at the surface. On the other hand, a warm humid wind that's above freezing will dramatically increase the chance of wet-snow avalanching. Moderate winds pick up loose snow and transport it. Watch for signs of drifting and possible slab formation. Strong winds will scour any large areas of snow, depleting the snowcover on the windward side of a mountain and depositing slab, often hard slab, in smaller pockets and depressions. Don't underestimate how fast strong winds can deposit snow on a lee slope.

Critical   — *moderate or strong wind*
— *cracking and settling of*
  snow

137

Air temperature

Very cold, below −15°C. Settlement is very slow. In a shallow snowpack recrystallization will occur. Check the amount of depth hoar in the snowpack. Bonding of new snow to the old snow surface remains weak when both layers are very cold, particularly if the old snow surface is a cold crust and the new snow is cold cohesionless grains. During extreme cold over prolonged periods with little snowfall, every layer in the snowpack loses strength with the result that avalanches can occur without any apparent reason.

Cold, −2°C to −15°C. Metamorphism proceeds more rapidly; watch for sluffs. Avalanches fall during or shortly after a storm. The snowpack then stabilizes and the danger recedes until the next storm.

Warm, −1°C and above. Rapid changes occur in the snowpack. If the air temperature remains close to freezing the snowpack will stabilize quickly. If it rise above freezing point wet snow avalanche hazard will develop. Check the depth of wet snow — twenty centimetres or more is dangerous — and note whether the snow freezes overnight. Cloudy days when little long wave radiation is lost to space will often set off a cycle of wet snow avalanching in early spring when previous clear sunny days have resulted in little or no activity.

Critical — *rapid rise in temperature*
— *above freezing temperatures*
— *sun on slope under consideration*
— *sun with hazy sky*
— *temperature inversions*

Humidity It's believed that high relative humidity encourages the formation of slab; it allows snow particles to be carried greater distances without subliming before they are deposited.

Critical — *High relative humidity during snowfall or during periods of moderate and strong winds.*

3. What will happen to me if the slope avalanches?

Depth of avalanche What depth of snow is likely to slide? How deep are the sliding layers in the snowpack? A few centimetres of snow are not significant if there is a long, almost flat runout, but could be fatal if there is an open crevasse waiting for the victim below.

Critical — *deep weak layers in snow pack*
— *foot penetration greater than 60 cm*

Type of avalanche Loose snow or slab? Wet or Dry? Will the whole slope slide at once?

Critical — *stiff slab above weak layers*
— *slope has not avalanched recently*

Terrain How large is the slope you are looking at. What is above? What is at the bottom? How deep will the snow pile up at the bottom? Are there cliff bands below?

Critical — *long open slope above*
— *restricted deposition zone*
— *drop-off below*
— *trees to wrap around*

4. Will conditions get worse?

This depends upon the present stability of the snowpack and what is happening to the weather. If you don't have a current weather forecast then you'll have to rely on your own observations. Obviously, any great change must be considered significant. Is it warming up? If so, what will the snow be like later on today, or tomorrow? Has it started to snow? How much and how fast? Is it accompanied by a strong wind?

Critical — *continuing snowfall*
— *increasing temperature*
— *strong wind*

Hazard Evaluation Summary

1. Could the slope produce avalanches?

Is the slope steep enough to slide?

Critical — *slopes greater than 30°*
— *variations in incline*
— *cliff bands.*

What's the orientation of the slope to wind?

Critical — *lee slopes*

What's the orientation of the slope to sun?

Critical — *S and SW slopes exposed to strong radiation*
— *first major thaw of spring*

What's the nature of the slope?

Critical — *open slopes*
— *thin forest*
— *confined slide path*
— *gully or bowl*
— *weak areas (Weak Spots) which might initiate failure*

2. Is the snow stable? Could it fail?

How deep is the snowpack?

Are there any signs of avalanche activity?

What layers are there in the snowpack?

Critical — *very hard or soft layers*
— *weak bond between layers*
— *30 cm or more snow above weak layer*
— *loose, cold snow*
— *wet snow*

How much fresh snow has fallen?

Critical — *snowfall greater than 2 cm per hour*
— *new snow depth greater than 30 cm*
— *slow settlement of new snow*
— *very light or very heavy snow*
— *heavily rimed crystals, graupel*

— *heavy stiff layer above a light weak layer*
— *heavy rain*
— *easy shovel test on new snow layer or Rutschblock fails when stepped on*

Wind

Critical — *moderate or strong wind*
— *cracking and settling of snow*

Air temperature

Critical — *rapid rise in temperature*
— *above freezing temperatures*
— *sun on slope under consideration*
— *sun with hazy sky*
— *temperature inversions*

Humidity

Critical — *High relative humidity during snowfall or during periods of moderate and strong wind.*

3. What will happen to me if the slope avalanches?

Depth of avalanche

Critical — *deep weak layers in snow pack*
— *foot penetration greater than 60 cm*

Type of avalanche

Critical — *stiff slab above weak layers*
— *slope has not avalanched recently*

Terrain

Critical — *long open slope above*
— *restricted deposition zone*
— *drop-off below*
— *trees to wrap around*

4. Will conditions get worse?

Critical — *continuing snowfall*
— *increasing temperature*
— *strong wind*

Fig. 8.1 Skiing deep powder in the backcountry requires good technique, the ability to evaluate snow stability and the practice of safe skiing techniques. Photo by Alf Skrastins.

8

Reducing the Odds

So far we have not addressed the needs of the backcountry powder-hound who deliberately seeks deep powder in avalanche terrain.

In order to ski "the steep and the deep" you are no longer trying to identify unstable slopes so you can avoid them, you are trying to find stable ones so you can ski them.

While we can take some comfort from the statement made by avalanche guru Ed LaChapelle that *"the snow is stable 90% of the time"*, there will always be risk when skiing steep slopes in the backcountry.

How can you reduce the risk to an acceptable minimum while still enjoying a good days' skiing?

If you are a serious deep powder hound you will learn to distinguish the good days from the bad, to observe current snow conditions, to evaluate snow stability from a few simple tests, to recognize signs of instability and, perhaps the most important factor in reducing the odds, you will practice safe skiing techniques.

Some Important Considerations

Many of the tip and techniques described in this chapter have already been covered in the chapters on "Observing Snow Conditions" "Recognizing Avalanche Terrain" and "Hazard Evaluation". Although I will cover some of the points again, you should review these chapters for applicable material and refer to the chapter on "Observing Snow Conditions" for a description of the tests for snow stability.

Risk

A discussion on evaluating snow stability would not be complete without some mention of risk. In the introduction I state that *"Only by recognizing risk can you use your knowledge and experience to reduce that risk"*. It can be further argued that whatever your personal acceptable level of risk the potential reward must always outweigh the risk. In other words don't stick your neck out for a run or two of lousy skiing. Save all of your "nine lives" (hopefully more) for those occasional perfect days.

Everyone has a different tolerance for risk, from the risk-seeker who skis steep slopes regardless of conditions to the person with a low tolerance for risk who will only venture onto steeper slopes when the snowpack is indisputably stable.

When skiing with a large group or with companions who are better skiers, you should avoid being pressured into accepting more risk than you really want to tolerate. Be aware of your companions attitude to risk and make adjustments on the conservative side if necessary.

Your Skiing Companions

Your choice of skiing companions is an important factor in the pursuit of safe skiing. The riskier the skiing the more critical it is to know their skiing ability and experience, their tolerance for risk and their potential behaviour in an emergency. Ideally you should ski with a small group of compan-

Fig. 8.2 It is good skiing practice to start at one side of the slope and work you way across, keeping the tracks as close together as possible. Photo by Bruce Jamieson.

ions of similar ability and with similar tolerance for risk. If you ski with a large group you will have to be much more conservative in your choice of slope as it is much more difficult to apply the principles of safe skiing to a big group.

The ideal group size is one which is small enough to be manageable and large enough to be effective in the event of an avalanche rescue. Four is a good number. Skiing alone leaves no margin for error and is not a good idea in avalanche terrain.

Ability

Because a good skier making smooth turns stresses a slope much less than a falling skier, you should match your skiing ability with the steepness and stability of the slopes you ski. A skier who has a tendency to "crash and burn" on steep slopes should not ski steep powder of dubious stability. There are some experts who consider that to ski deep powder in marginal conditions you should be able to "parallel" ski, as "telemarking" puts a greater stress on the snow!

Before You Go

Safety Equipment

It is probably stating the obvious to point out that if you are a deep-powder fanatic you should possess, carry and know how to use basic safety and rescue equipment. If you get into trouble, self rescue is your only hope. Make sure that all your party have working avalanche beacons and are proficient in their use.

Local Knowledge

Your margin of safety will be much higher if you ski slopes you know well, than if you ski a new area. If you ski regularly in the same area over a period of years you will learn which slopes can be safely skied in different snow conditions and which slopes are prone to avalanching. You will get a feel for the area so that your observations of conditions will become keener. The importance of local knowledge cannot be overstated.

Form an Opinion on Snow Stability

If you are skiing in your local area and have followed the build-up of the snowpack and recent changes in weather you should be able to form an opinion, no matter how rough, about current snow stability. Build up an overall picture as the winter progresses and revise and refine this picture every time

you go skiing. Choose your destination for the day with this picture in mind, and as you approach your chosen slopes compare your stability prediction with actual snow conditions. Do not let your desire to ski a slope interfere with your evaluation of its stability

Snow, Avalanche and Weather Reports

In many areas you can obtain up-to-date avalanche forecasts prepared by professional forecasters. While these reports are usually for large regions or even for whole mountain areas, in times of high or extreme instability they will sound a warning bell. They will often indicate the conditions which are causing instability such as persistent buried surface hoar or wind loaded slopes of a certain aspect. Along with a call to the weather office a call to your nearest avalanche forecast centre or to park rangers and wardens is one of the prerequisites for safe skiing.

Wait for the Right Conditions

Successful (surviving) extreme skiers make meticulous preparations and wait for exactly the right conditions before making their descent. Following their example, you should wait for the right conditions before skiing a particular slope or gully. Be flexible in your choice of slopes; if conditions are not right go somewhere else. Timing is everything!

Fig. 8.3 Skiing the Polaris Bowl, near Fernie, British Columbia, requires that you wait for the right conditions. Photo by Bruce Jamieson.

Snowcraft

Snowcraft is a little used term for an almost lost art. Anchorage avalanche educator, Doug Fesler, calls it "wearing your avalanche eyeballs" Like navigation it is the art of observing, storing and compiling into a picture a multitude of minute details. Observation is the key to safe travel through avalanche terrain and a major factor in evaluating the stability of a snow slope.

Look for recent avalanche activity, settling of the snowpack or cracks in the surface due to settlement. Feel the snow with your skis to detect any changes to hardness or texture. If you are following in the tracks of other skiers, step out of the trail occasionally. If there is fresh snow, check the depth as you ascend and evaluate how well it is bonded to the old snow surface. Look for signs of drifting. What has been the direction of the wind recently? Keep you eyes open and you senses alert. Gather as much information as you can.

A good guide depends largely on "feel". The "feel" of the snow beneath his skis as he turns and a "sense" of terrain. His built-in wealth of experience attunes him to anticipate potential problems as he skis various types of terrain just as a good driver senses potentially dangerous situations developing around him on the highway.

Weather

Don't forget to observe the weather. Changes in weather, particularly heavy snowfall, current wind speed and direction or a sudden rise in temperature all have an important effect on snow stability.

Test Slopes

Small, steep slopes along your route will give some indication of stability. Try to ski them off or jump on the top of them. Jump on cornices as long as you can do it safely. A good sized chunk of cornice rolling down a slope without triggering a slide will give you a lot of confidence in a slope's stability.

Ski cutting the top of large slopes is a much dicier business and should be done with caution. Never ski cut below a cornice. A snowboarder became the first snowboard avalanche fatality in Canada by doing this.

Snowpits

Dig a snowpit on a test slope in a safe location. It is usually not necessary for the back-country skier to dig more than about 1.5 - 2 m deep. You really have no way of evaluating deep instability and if deep instability is forecast by your local avalanche warning centre you should be skiing somewhere else; somewhere safe.

According to Bruce Tremper, a professional stability forecaster, *"The name of the game is to dig a pit in the most representative spot you can choose without getting killed"*. You may have to settle for a smaller test slope, and try to extrapolate the results to the larger slope, or work your way in towards the middle of the larger slope, digging several quick pits and retreating if there is any indication of instability.

In order to get reliable results, take care when choosing your snowpit locations. Stay away from trees; avoid drifts or ridges where the wind may have altered the layering of the snowpack; be aware of rockbands, buried bush or other shallow spots and avoid breaks or transitions in the slope. The ideal location is in the middle of a steep, open slope!

As you dig, pay attention to the consistency of the snow. You can learn a lot about the composition of the snowpack during the digging process.

Feel the snow with your gloved hand to get an idea what layers are present in the snowpack. Don't bother with brushes or credit cards or with looking at the snow crystals with a magnifying glass. All you are trying to see is the overall picture. Look for the weakest layer and trying to estimate how well it is bonded to the adjacent layers.

Shovel Shear Test

Do a Shovel Shear test looking for weak layers, especially layers of buried surface hoar. Remember that the shovel shear test is a good way to identify weak layers in the snowpack but a poor way to evaluate its stability. Review the procedure on page 103 and make sure you know how to do it correctly. The way you cut the back of the column is critical.

Loaded Column Test

Do a Loaded Column test to identify the weakest layer and to get an idea of how much weight can be applied to the snow before it fails.

Rutschblock Test

Do a Rutschblock test as a practical evaluation of stability and as a means of filling in your snowpit as a courtesy to other skiers.

If you find no significant instability work your way out onto the edge of the slope you wish to ski, probing with ski poles as you go to determine if the consistency of the snow and the makeup of the layers remains the same. Do another quick series of tests. Depending on what you find you may wish to stick you nose farther out onto the slope, or you may decide to retreat.

Fig. 8.4 It is not "safe skiing" to start you run half-way up a gully like these early-season skiers. Although they have chosen a reasonable climbing line up the treed ridge on the left, they chose to begin their run at the bottom of the wind-loaded gully with a substantial collection area above. The slopes avalanched later in the day, covering their tracks with about a metre of snow.

Procedure for Stability Evaluation

— Form an opinion on current stability from your home.

— Call the avalanche hotline for your area.

— Pick the area in which to go skiing based on the above opinion.

— Observe slopes visible from the road as you drive to your destination.

— Decide the slope you are going to ski when you get to the area and have had a chance to evaluate stability.

— Determine the angle of your intended slope. Is it 35° or steeper?

— Practice the fundamentals of snowcraft.

— Jump on small, steep test slopes along the route to see if they slide.

— Jump on cornices as long as you can do it safely.

— Dig a snowpit pit on a test slope in a safe location.

— Pay attention to snow consistency as you dig.

— Run a gloved hand down the pit wall to get an idea of layering.

— Look for the weakest layers.

— Do a Shovel Shear test to identify weak layers.

— Do a Loaded Column test to identify the weakest layer and to estimate how much weight can be applied to the snow before it fails.

— Do a Rutschblock test as a practical evaluation of stability.

— Probing with ski poles as you climb to the top of your chosen slope to determine if the consistency of the snow and the makeup of the layers remains the same.

— If in doubt do another quick series of tests.

— Practice "Safe Skiing" techniques.

Safe Skiing

'The first rule of thumb in safe skiing is, if your partner wants to ski first ...let him!"
Brad Meiklejohn

After stability evaluation the best way of "Reducing the Odds" is to practice safe skiing techniques. There is one overriding rule for safe skiing and that is; **never expose more than one skier at a time to avalanche danger**. The following are pointers gathered from ski guides, avalanche professionals, extreme skiers and backcountry ski fanatics.

One thing all these people have in common is that they are willing to turn around and go home if they become uncomfortable about the level of risk.

Managing your party

— Plan your descent. Decide where on the slope you will put the first track, who will ski first, which side of the first track the second skier will ski and how far down the slope you will ski before stopping to regroup. Stop at the very edge of the slope or ski right to the bottom.

— If the entire run is not visible, stop (to the side) at any changes in steepness or direction and ski the new section as a separate slope.

— Ski one at a time and watch each skier for the entire run. Don't start until the previous skier is out of the way. Skiing one at a time keeps the stress on a slope to a minimum.

— Don't ski above one an other. Take care when tree skiing or skiing rolls and bumps not to ski above you partner. Move well to one side or to a safe position following your run.

— Use the buddy system and stay within sight or sound of your buddy at all times

Skiing the slope

— Start the day by skiing easier angled slopes and work your way onto the steeper slopes. Ski treed slopes before open ones.

— Typically the first run of the day is always a safe run with several test locations for stability evaluations; a small steep roll or short commonly wind-loaded slope. Continue to sniff around, being constantly aware of changing weather and snow conditions.

— Start skiing a slope at the sides, working towards the centre on successive runs.

— Ski on ridges instead of bowls; stay out of gullies and avoid skiing slopes which channel into gullies; be alert for terrain traps.

— Enter the slope at the top rather than at the sides. Don't ski in from the side below a cornice.

— Take a good look at the slope and consider the possibility of "weak spots". Ski where the snowpack appears to be deepest, avoiding possible "weak spots" In depth hoar conditions stay away from rocks which may be trigger points.

— Ski as smoothly as possible and in control. Sit down rather than crash.

— Ski the same slopes as often as you can throughout the season. This not only gives you an intimate knowledge of the terrain, but also ski packs the snow, reducing its potential for sliding.

— Put your climbing track on safe, low-angled slopes. Climbing straight up on foot should only be done on the most stable slopes.

— A new lesson learned from heli-skiing is to look well above and contemplate triggering an avalanche that starts a long distance away.

146

Weak Spots

It is possible that, on any given slope, the strength of a buried weak layer, or of the snowpack itself, may vary from place to place.

Consider a slope covered with a certain depth of snow. If the slope were perfectly even , you would expect the snowpack to be uniform across the slope. However, if the slope is uneven or if there are buried rocks or brush, then the temperature gradient in those areas will be different and the snowpack will no longer be uniform. In climates where recrystallization is taking place such areas may be weaker and potentially less stable due to the higher rate of recrystallization. These areas are called "weak spots"

In studying a number of slab avalanches which have been triggered by a person adding stress to a weak layer, it has been noticed that the initial rupture of the slab usually begins in a localized area where the weak layer is at its weakest.

Once failure occurs at the "weak spot", the fracture propagates rapidly throughout the slab into areas of stronger snow; into snow which your companions may have safely descended.

The Implications of "Weak Spots"

The farther down the weak layer is in the snowpack, the less likely you are to trigger an avalanche, therefore you should try to ski where the snow cover is deepest and keep away from rocks or brush protruding from the snow. On suspect slopes, follow the exact line taken by the person in front.

Remember that the more you concentrate your weight in a small area the more stress you transmit to the snowpack. A snowboarder will add less stress to a weak layer than will a person on skis. Taking your skis off and walking down a slope is a dubious technique when slab conditions are suspected.

The old concept of moving between "islands of safety" needs revising to stress that the "islands" should be large and solid. A substantial clump of trees or a solid rock buttress, rather than insubstantial objects such as small trees or brush sticking up through the snow.

Fig. 8.5 Snow weakened by recrystallization in the vicinity of the partially buried rocks may have been the "weak spot" which allowed the skier to trigger this slide. Note that the fracture line extends up into the area the skier had skied without release occuring. The right-hand photo shows the extent of the buried rocks.
Photos by Tom Fankhanel.

9

Routefinding

Nowhere is the skill of routefinding more important than in avalanche country. The route must not only be speedy and require the minimum of effort, but also must be safe from avalanches. Good routefinding is learned by experience; by following experienced leaders through a variety of terrain in all weather conditions. It depends upon pre-planning, careful observation, a knowledge of land forms and snow conditions and upon the ability to make sensible decisions based upon all the available information. Because evaluation of all the factors which may lead to an avalanche is a very complex subject and one which a normal skiing or climbing party is ill equipped to make, always allow a wide margin of safety when making a routefinding decision.

Fig. 9.1 The importance of good routefinding cannot be overstressed. These snowshoers have descended from the ridge and are re-ascending to a col on the left. Would you have taken the same route, knowing that conditions were unstable? Photo by Roland V. Emetaz, Courtesy U.S. Forest Service.

Choosing a Safe Route

It's impossible to write about routefinding without also considering the impending pressures facing a party in the backcountry. These pressures, whether real or imaginary, tend to bias decisions in a variety of ways. Such concerns include sickness and injury, fatigue, time constraints and weather conditions. Often they're used to justify a certain course of action:

— *"We decided to hug the left side of the valley so that we wouldn't lose elevation or time."*

— *"Darkness was coming, so we pressed on to the pass."*

— *"I had to be back at work by Monday morning."*

— *"We had planned the trip for three years and we were not about to throw it all away because of one storm."*

Fig. 9.2 Convex slopes, such as this one in Jasper National Park, Canadian Rockies, are potentially dangerous and should be traversed one at a time and as high up the slope as possible.

In each of the above cases, the victims felt compelled to make a decision based upon factors which they perceived as important. When making routefinding decisions identify the assumptions upon which decisions are being made and get into the habit of verifying them. Ask yourself *"Do we really need to reach that goal today? Does it really matter if I'm late for work on Monday? What are the possible consequences of my decision to carry on?"*

Other assumptions which presume a situation is safe are based upon incomplete information:

— *"We didn't think the slope was steep enough to slide so we cut across it."*

— *"We followed the tracks of another party up the mountain figuring that if they made it, we could make it."*

— *"We thought that we would be safe following a route through the trees."*

— *"We took every precaution; each man carried a rescue beacon, a probe, and a shovel, and we spread out while crossing the slope."*

— *"The snow ranger said that the hazard was rated low to moderate, so we didn't expect to get caught."*

Fig. 9.3 When slab is suspected, be very careful when skiing over small rolls in the terrain. This small slope in the Esplanades, British Columbia was an anomaly in otherwise gentle terrain.

In each case, the victims decided to cross a slope assuming that it was safe. In each case the victims triggered the avalanche which buried them. So ask yourself, *"What can go wrong? Is there an error in my reasoning? Upon what assumptions am I basing my decision?"* Consider the first example. In March of 1979, three Alaskans were travelling on snowshoes along a broad valley close to the steep slopes of the mountain to their right. At the time of the accident they had left the security of the flat valley floor and were cutting across a gentle slope with only a 12° incline. Suddenly the snowpack settled with a "whumph"; the steeper slope to their right fractured 10 m above them and came pouring down burying two of the men completely. Unknown to the party, a layer of depth hoar 8 cm thick lay buried half a metre beneath the snow surface. In addition, 70 km per hour winds the night before had significantly loaded the slope. These two factors combined with the sudden new weight of three men travelling along the foot of the slope were enough to initiate failure and the slope avalanched. *"We didn't think the slope was steep enough to slide"* was their response. In retrospect they might have said, *"We didn't think...enough about the consequences of our actions."*

False reasoning led the victims to believe the slope was safe. They had failed to consider the effect of a strong wind loading fresh snow onto the slope, the possibility of a sliding layer within the snowpack and the configuration of the slope above them. Their decision to continue following along the base of the mountain was based upon only one item of information — slope angle — and even then they failed to fully explore the evidence before them. They simply lacked the knowledge of what information to look for and how to evaluate it.

Decision-making

You've spent the better part of the day heading toward your objective, a mountain pass, still some 2 km distant. The other two members of your group want to reach the pass before darkness falls. You're tired; breaking trail through knee-deep snow has been difficult. The ridge route you've been following bends abruptly to the east and ends at the bottom of a steep snow-cushioned slope rimmed by a large cornice. Your objective is on the other side. A light breeze is picking up out of the south-east, but the sky is still clear except for a scattering of pink mare's tails high overhead. What should you do?

If you haven't done so already, it's time to start asking yourself — and your group — some important questions:

Why am I here?

This question really asks *"What are objectives to be achieved?"* Every decision needs to be measured against a yardstick of purpose. The purpose may be to climb a certain peak. It may be to have a good time and get some exercise. It may be to hone climbing skills. Safety is usually an unspoken objective.

What is the problem?

In the example of the group heading towards the mountain pass, the problem starts to surface when the good ridge route abruptly terminates below the ominous looking snow slope. Is it safe to proceed farther? The problem rapidly begins to compound itself when you take into consideration other impending factors such as group fatigue, approaching darkness, goal-oriented pressure, deteriorating weather, and alternative routes. The problem now becomes not only the original problem, but all of its consequential ramifications.

What are the alternatives?

Consider your options in terms of your trip objectives. In this case your options are:

— *Continue on.*

— *Stay put.*

— *Turn around and backtrack.*

— *Take an alternative route.*

Fig. 9.4 White River Canyon in Oregon has the potential for many avalanche accidents. The ski trail shown in the photograph is routed under a steep cornice-hung, lee slope. Photo by Steve Couche.

Fig .9.5 The route to the col at the top left of the photograph follows the bench between the crevasses and the icefall on the east face of Mountain Balfour, Canadian Rockies. On some occasions, the narrow passage is swept by snow and ice avalanches.

What are the probable consequences of these alternatives

Which alternative gives you the best chance of success as measured by your objectives? If you carry on what are your chances of getting caught, buried, or killed? Are you willing to bet your life on your decision? The real question is, *"Is it worth it?"*

What information is available to me?

In essence, all you've observed in your surroundings, everything you've learned about weather and snow mechanics. Only by educating yourself can you expect to understand the physical processes at play and so sort out the information which is relevant.

What are the impending pressures?

This question also asks *"Are these pressures really important?"* Many times people tend to imagine the importance of a belief, which, when viewed in retrospect, becomes meaningless. Try to sort out those impending pressures which have real significance from those which do not. Your boss would rather have you back at work on Tuesday than go to your funeral on Thursday.

What assumptions am I making?

Don't make decisions based upon assumptions which you haven't verified. When in doubt, check it out. What thinking person doesn't travel through avalanche terrain without doubts?

Decisions on safe route selection must be based upon facts and not upon assumptions.

Fig. 9.6 A selection of routefinding problems showing good and bad
routes. Illustrations from the Avalanche Handbook.

Crossing a Suspect Slope

The first thing to do if faced with crossing a suspect slope is to look for another route which will avoid the slope completely.

When it really is impossible to avoid the slide area, consider where the likely trigger zone might be. A wide slope can have several distinctly different trigger zones, each of which can initiate an avalanche either locally or over the entire slope. Avalanches often start at the steepest point on a convex slope, or at some discontinuity across a slope such as rocks, a rock band or clumps of trees. Slab avalanches can be triggered from way below the crown line and in very unstable conditions from relatively flat ground below a slope. Remember also when investigating snow conditions, that a long slope will have different snow conditions at the top than at the bottom.

If you're standing on safe ground level with a potential starting zone you should either climb to the very top of the slope or drop well down into the runout zone. This may seem like a lot of effort for a tired party, but is infinitely preferable to conducting an avalanche search and rescue operation. If you can't ascend or descend on safe slopes because of impenetrable timber or rock bands, the riskier alternative is to use the side of the suspect slope. If it's too steep for side stepping, take your skis off and walk.

When crossing the runout zone of a wide avalanche gully space yourselves at least 50 m apart and decide on a point of no return in case a slide starts above you. Post a spotter to warn of incipient slides. After your group has crossed, continue far enough along the trail to be completely clear of any possible avalanche before stopping.

Fig. 9.7 The runout zone of wide avalanche gullies can be safely crossed when hazard is low or moderate. If hazard is high or extreme, consider how far the debris may run and take all possible precautions.

The procedure for crossing a potential avalanche slope is quite different. Try to pick a line where you can traverse downhill; if possible a line which will take you in a series of short traverses from one point of safety to another such as large rocks or a thick clump of trees. It maybe that your point of safety is the discontinuity across which the avalanche fails, in which case there is some comfort in knowing that you're at the very top of the slide when it starts and therefore have a good chance of emerging unscathed.

The worst thing you can do is undercut the snow by traversing horizontally across a slope. Try to avoid making turns; the extra force which is applied when weighting the ski in preparation for the turn and the carving action of the turn itself could be the trigger which releases the slide.

With the rest of the party watching, **expose only one person at a time to danger**. Never assume that because a slope didn't slide when the first person was crossing that it's safe for the rest of the party to cross en masse; the additional weight of several skiers together could be more than enough to initiate release. Also bear in mind that a slope may still release after several individual skiers have crossed it. On reaching safe ground, the first skiers should wait and watch from a safe spot until the whole party is over. Of course, if the slope is very wide exposing one person at a time is not practical. In this case travel at least 100 metres apart.

Climbers, likewise, should cross suspect slopes one at a time, being careful not to create a trench in the snow and so undercut a slab. Only rope up if the distance is short and good static belays are available. When crossing a wide slope you have to decide whether the risk of the slope avalanching is greater than the risk of falling. If the answer is yes, and static belays are not available, cross the slope one person at a time **unroped**.

In the event of an avalanche, using a rope can seriously hinder your chances of getting out alive: it tangles you up preventing you from making swimming motions, and pulls you down even deeper into the moving snow. Moreover, other members of the group, not originally caught in the avalanche, may be pulled into it.

Fig. 9.8 This photograph illustrates the wrong way to cross potential avalanche slopes. The wind-etched surface is probably safe, but what are conditions like on far side of the ridge Photo by Roland V. Emetaz, courtesy U.S. Forest Service.

Before crossing a suspect slope fasten your parka and pull up the hood, put on mitts, remove safety straps if they're being used, take your hands out of wrist loops, undo the belly band of your pack and ensure that rescue beacons are switched on or that avalanche cords are deployed. Alpine bindings should be set loose enough to kick out of. Pin bindings and cross-country cable bindings can be loosened satisfactorily, but Nordic Norm bindings pose more of a problem because they hold the boot very firmly to the ski and can't be loosened. The best suggestion I have heard of so far is to slacken the laces of the ski boot.

Plan ahead of time what you're going to do if the snow does release; maybe if you have a good downward traverse there's a chance of skiing to the side. But supposing you can't ski — and the chances are you won't be able to — what then? The first few seconds of mentally rehearsed action on your part may make the difference between survival and death.

Fig. 9.9 Expose only one person at a time to danger when crossing steep slopes. This most important rule is often ignored. Note the cornice above and wind drifting around trees. Photo by Roland V. Emetaz, courtesy U.S. Forest Service.

What to do if Avalanched

When learning snowcraft and studying its application to avalanches you'll probably become over cautious for a time. Accident reports in the local press will serve as a reminder that the danger is very real. As your knowledge increases, however, you'll tend to become overconfident in your ability to judge slopes in marginal conditions. In other words, the greater your experience the closer you'll try to approach that narrow dividing line between stability and instability. This may be done unconsciously; because you've crossed many slopes which didn't slide, you begin to assume that all similar slopes are safe. The chances are that one day you'll be caught in an avalanche. What can you do to help yourself if you do get caught?

Hopefully you'll be aware that the slope you're crossing is potentially dangerous and will be crossing one at a time with at least one other person watching. You will have made sure your transceiver is turned on or your avalanche cord is deployed and will have loosened safety straps, donned hat, mitts and anorak and chosen the best possible line for crossing.

When the snow starts to slide make a quick decision. Can I ski out of it or not? This will depend on your ability as a skier, the depth of snow, steepness of the slope and the configuration of the avalanche path. If you can, ski towards the edge of the slide where the snow is moving more slowly and may be shallower. At Bridger Bowl ski area in Montana, a patrolman who was caught in a dry soft slab avalanche reported that, *"When the slide hit, I tried to get my skis pointed straight down the hill, but didn't have much luck due to the boiling of the snow."* One problem with slab avalanches is that as soon as the snow breaks up and loses its internal cohesion your skis sink deeper into the snow making it very difficult to force the tips up to the surface. Also the jarring drop and sudden movement of the slope will throw all but the best skiers off balance.

Fight for your life.

Shout out so your companions know you are in trouble.

Throw away your ski poles; you should already be free of the wrist loops. A ski instructor in Jackson, *"tried to make swimming motions, but his ski poles kept pulling him down."* He *"tried to get his hands to his face to make a breathing pocket, but his poles frustrated his effort."*

Kick off your skis. Getting rid of your skis is of prime importance; you'll have very little chance of fighting your way to the surface if you are constantly being dragged down and twisted by the leverage of snow on your skis. The same patrolman at Bridger Bowl who tried to ski out of the avalanche then, *"tried swimming, but this is very difficult to accomplish with skis on, for the instant they are pulled out of parallel with the fall line the feet are pulled uphill with respect to the rest of the body, causing a roll."* He also observed, *"that the snow set up on stopping, even though it was fairly dry".*

Grab at trees or rocks. In the early stages of the slide you may be able to arrest your downward plunge.

Wriggle free of your pack. If you are wearing a heavy pack your belly band should already be undone.

Swim. Try to stay on the surface of the snow by pumping your legs up and down in a treading water motion and by dog paddling with your arms. A skier in the Colorado Rockies describes the technique. *"I worked myself into a sitting position, with my feet downhill, and tried to swim as if treading water. This seemed to work, and I immediately started to rise in the snow."* A companion *"was knocked forward by the slide and swam on his stomach, head downhill, as though he was doing a breast stroke."* In this same avalanche incident another skier was saved because a section of his avalanche cord remained on the surface. If you feel your feet touch the ground give a hard push and try to pop out onto the surface.

A large avalanche in Bridger Bowl caught 5 skiers but *"By swimming all managed to stay near the surface of the slide."* A member of the Ski Patrol *"noted that when he started to swim, he felt his feet swing below his head, and the rest of his body popped right out of the slide. As the avalanche ran over the cliff, he was buried again, but by "swimming" he was able to regain the surface."*

Gerald Seligman recounts the case of a Zermatt guide, *"who, being thrown down by a dry powder snow avalanche, rolled over and over sideways until he emerged at the side of the avalanche, twelve feet in a more or less horizontal distance from where he had been caught."* More modern writers, particularly those who have skied in the Alps , have also mentioned this technique. It appears that the initial twist of the feet releases the safety bindings and initiates the first roll. It may be the answer to escaping from a small slide where you don't have time to get into a swimming position.

Shut your mouth as soon as your head goes under and try to hold your breath for as long as possible. A Banff mountain guide who was caught in a soft slab, *"took a breath and immediately my windpipe was blocked by snow. Further breathing was impossible. Fortunately after a few seconds the snow melted enough for me to cough out the plug of snow and take another breath as my head came clear. I held my breath while under the snow until my head came clear again."* Many victims have died from suffocation in this manner.

Get into a sitting position facing downhill, with your legs out in front and together. You can only do this if you've managed to stay on the surface. As the snow stops you are in a position to stand up and let the snow coming from behind fill in around you. Put one hand in front of your face and the other above your head if you think you're going to be buried. Shake your head from side to side in an effort to clear an air space.

Make a last desperate effort to pop yourself out if you're below the surface when the slide starts to slow down.

Make a breathing space in front of your nose and mouth with one hand and push the other one towards where you think the surface is. Several victims have been found quickly because a hand was seen sticking out of the snow. One ski tourer who survived after 9 hours of burial reported that, *"My arm was over my head. That's probably what saved me. It created a little air pocket about twice the size of my head."* Another ski patroller credits moving his head from side to side with saving his life, *"As the snow from above buried me, I managed to move my head enough to form a small air pocket".* An accident involving two skiers in Big Cottonwood Canyon, Utah, serves as another reminder. *"Both were located, by Pieps, beneath 4 feet of snow. One victim was uncovered in 20 minutes, having been buried upside down with no airspace; he was dead. The other was uncovered in 25 minutes, hands in front of face and alive".* Another suggestion is to try to attain a crouching position, hands in front of the face like a boxer. Only rarely, if not buried too deeply in loose recrystallized snow, is it possible to crawl out from under the debris.

When the Snow Comes to Rest

In most slides the snow sets up like cement on coming to rest, and even if you are only partially buried it may be difficult, even impossible, to dig yourself out. It's very unlikely that you can help yourself if completely buried.

Don't shout unless you hear rescuers immediately above you; sound will not penetrate through more than a few cm of snow.

Don't struggle to free yourself; you will only be wasting energy and precious oxygen.

Try to relax and if you feel yourself about to pass out don't fight it. The respiration of an unconscious person is shallower, their pulse rate declines and the body temperature is lowered, all of which reduce the amount of oxygen needed.

The following extract is taken from "The Avalanche Hunters" by Monty Atwater and is probably the most explicit account of how it feels to be caught in an avalanche ever written.

"When a soft slab breaks loose it crumbles internally, losing all its cohesion and flotation. I simply fell through it until my skis hit the hard base of the old snow underneath. Now the snow along the wall of the gully began to curl back towards the main current, taking me with it. I was knee deep in boiling snow, then waist deep, then neck deep. Through ankles and knees I felt my skis drift onto the fall line. But I was still erect, still on top of them. The books tell you, If you're caught in an avalanche, try to ski out of it. With mine trapped under six feet of snow I wasn't skiing out of anything. I wondered what was going to happen when it came time to make that right-angle turn into Corkscrew.

Very fast and very suddenly I made two forward somersaults, like a pair of pants in a dryer. At the end of each revolution the avalanche smashed me hard against the base. It was like a man swinging a sack full of ice against a rock to break it into smaller pieces. Fortunately I took both shocks on the derriere, not on some more vulnerable spot. There was no pain, just a jolt that wrenched a grunt out of me each time. At this moment, the avalanche had taken my skis off for me and in doing so had spared my life, by giving up the leverage with which it could twist me into a pretzel. I didn't know my skis were gone and I don't remember the turn into Corkscrew. I was all the way under by then.

If my memories of this avalanche seem to be rather clear and detailed, it was a memorable occasion. I was a trained observer. In my few years at Alta as a pro-

fessional avalanche hunter I'd done a lot of thinking about this moment. I was thinking now and fighting for my life. However, my principal sensation was one of wild excitement.

Under the snow there was utter darkness instead of that radiance of sun and snow which is never so bright as directly after a storm. It was a churning, twisting darkness in which I was wrestled about as if by a million hands. I began to black out, a darkness that comes from within.

Suddenly I was on the surface again, in sunlight. I spat a wad of snow out of my mouth and took a deep breath. I thought, so that's why avalanche victims are always found with their mouths full of snow. You're fighting like a demon, mouth wide open to get more air, and the avalanche stuffs it with snow. I remembered another piece of advice in the books: Cover your mouth and nose. The next time I surfaced I got two breaths.

It happened several times: on top, take a breath, swim for the shore; underneath, cover up, curl into a ball. This seemed to go on for a long time, and I was beginning to black out again. Then I felt the snow cataract begin to slow down and squeeze.

At the mouth of Corkscrew the slope widens out and becomes gentle. The avalanche had swept me onto this slope. The squeezing was the result of the slowdown, with snow still pressing from behind. Whether from instinct or a last flicker of reason, I gave a tremendous heave, and the avalanche spat me onto the surface like the seed out of a grapefruit."

In summary, if caught in an avalanche which you cannot ski out of, get rid of your skis and poles, try to stay on the surface by making swimming motions, as the snow comes to a standstill make a breathing space in front of your head. Finally, relax and rely on your companions to dig you out.

Fig. 9.10 This large slab in the Bugaboos, British Columbia, fractured and collapsed but did not release. The slope had been skied the previous day. Photo by Jim Davies.

Fig. 10.1 Rescuers dig out one of the victims of the
1975 accident on Mount St. Helens. Photo by
Roland V. Emetaz, Courtesy U.S. Forest Service.

10

Rescue

December 11th was the first day of operations at the Sunshine Village Ski area. As usual at the beginning of the season the snowpack was unconsolidated and several of the steeper runs were closed. Three skiers alighting from the Standish chairlift started off in the direction of Bunkers Run, but when informed by the lift operator that the area was closed, appeared to ski off in another direction. As soon as they were out of sight of the lift operator they ducked under the roped fence, ignored a "No skiing" sign and entered Bunkers Run. As they skied down towards Donkey's Tail they passed several boundary poles and another sign that read "Danger - Avalanche Area Closed". Donkeys Tail is a short steep hillside overlooked by a crowded ski slope so there were plenty of people to witness what happened, including a group of ski instructors. The first skier got down the slope safely, but the second man fell about half way down. At the same time, the third man entering the steep slope triggered a small slide 10 metres wide by 30 metres long which was sufficient to knock the second man off his feet and bury him.

The ski instructors, on the scene in seconds, organized a hasty search and it was during the initial search that one of the rescuers scuffing among the debris had the good fortune to kick the victim's boot. Frantic digging uncovered the rest of his body; his head was 1.5 metres below the surface and he was not breathing. Fortunately, a few breaths of mouth-to-mouth resuscitation were sufficient to bring him round. Only seven minutes had elapsed since the time of the accident.

This skier was lucky; the avalanche was witnessed and searching started within a few seconds of his burial. Although he was found within a few minutes he was already unconscious. How much longer would he have lasted? *"A highly experienced ski tourer was killed in the Wasatch Mountains of Utah. Out of sight of his companions, he triggered a soft slab avalanche on a timbered slope, was carried to the runout, and was buried 4' deep. All party members carried rescue beacons and shovels. The victim was located and dug out in 15 minutes, but had died of suffocation."* Brain damage occurs about 4 minutes after the organ is deprived of oxygenated blood and after 8 to 10 minutes survival is unlikely even if breathing and circulation are restored.

Statistics indicate that the chance of survival diminishes rapidly to 50% in the first half hour and that few people survive if buried deeper than 2 metres. There is, of course, the occasional report of victims surviving for many hours, even days, under avalanche debris but in every case they had a large breathing space in front of their faces. Although survival time statistics are not very encouraging, it's important not to give up hope as was illustrated on Ben Nevis, Scotland in 1967. Two climbers had set out to climb No.4 Gully, an easy-angled route which on that morning was covered with a layer of fresh wet snow. About noon they were avalanched from just below the point where the gully narrowed. One of the climb-

Fig. 10.2 After 22 hours of burial in an avalanche on Beinn a'Bhurd, Robert Burnett is dug alive. This is the longest live burial ever recovered in the U.K. Photo by Hamish MacInnes.

ers ended up in a deep hole about four feet below the surface from which he finally extracted himself after struggling for several hours. Somehow he stumbled down in the dark to the CIC hut which he reached about 9:30 that night. A rescue party followed the survivors tracks back to the gully and began searching the area. They didn't have much hope of finding the other climber alive. About midnight one of the rescuers spotted the glint of an ice axe which on closer inspection had fingers curled around it. To their amazement muffled shouts were coming from beneath the snow. Against all odds, the climber had survived for twelve hours and was recovered weak but uninjured.

Unlike accidents in or near a downhill ski area where professional help is always available, **avalanche rescue in the backcountry depends upon the actions of the unburied survivors.** If outside help has to be called in then it's usually to recover a body.

Searching for Buried Skiers		
Method	Time to search 100 x 100 m area	Chance of success when buried 3 m or less
Coarse probe One pass	20 probers 4 hours	70%
Fine probe	20 probers 16 to 20 hours	100%
Dog, quick search	1 dog, half hour	90%
Dog, detailed search	1 dog, 1 - 2 hours	95%
Rescue beacons	1 person under 10 minutes	98%

Everyone who goes out into the mountains should know the basic procedures of back-country rescue. In Jasper National Park on February 15th, 1977, a man died because his friends didn't know what to do. Seven ski tourers out enjoying the powder slopes of Parker's Ridge were returning to Hilda Creek Hostel in the late afternoon. Five minutes before the hostel they came to a short steep slope about 30 m high which looked like fun. Unknown to the skiers the configuration of the land had allowed the prevailing wind to load the top of the slope while scouring snow from the bottom, leaving a dangerous slab hanging there unsupported. (The same innocuous looking slope had been the scene of another fatality ten years previously.) The first man, entering the slope from the side just below a small cornice, promptly fell face down on the hard slab and triggered a very small avalanche which rolled him down and buried him under 60 cm of snow. Unfortunately, the second man who up to that time had been watching the leader, had turned his head away at the crucial moment and so didn't see the accident or get any idea of where his friend might be buried. It was at this point that the skiers made a serious mistake: they all left the scene of the accident and returned to their cars for shovels. By the time they'd climbed back up and had started digging random holes in the debris vital minutes had slipped by. It was sheer bad luck they chose to dig in the wrong places. Had they spent the time immediately after the accident in organized probing with upturned poles they would have located the victim within 5 minutes and almost certainly have recovered him alive. As it was he was found some 2 hours later by Ginger, a Parks rescue dog.

Because time is the critical factor in any avalanche rescue, every available person should be used in the search. Unless help is only a few minutes away, wait for at least an hour before raising the alarm.

Of the three proven methods used to locate a buried person, the use of avalanche rescue beacons is by far the most effective. The table on page 164 outlines the three methods, time factors and chance of success.

Fig. 10.3 The dangerous slope at Parker's Ridge in the Canadian Rockies, Scene of 2 fatalities. The wind blows from right to left, loading upper slopes with wind-driven snow and scouring out the snow at the bottom of the slope. Photo by Jim Davies.

Organized Avalanche Rescue

A knowledge what happens during a formal rescue may help a touring party to improvise effectively during a back-country accident. Although you're not as well equipped as a professional rescue team you do have the advantage of being on the scene and, therefore, in the best position to effect a live recovery.

Formal rescue is considerably hampered by the time factors involved. Even for a well organized ski area it take several minutes to raise the alarm, 5 to 10 minutes to organize and get moving, 15 to 20 minutes to ride a lift and a few more minutes to reach the scene. Only the best organized ski areas can get a rescue team to their avalanche slopes within half an hour.

Most downhill areas have written rescue plans which spell out precisely what action should be taken after the alarm is raised and which personnel will lead the rescue. The key figure is the Rescue Leader or Rescue Co-ordinator who is in overall charge of the operation. It's his responsibility to arrange medical support, helicopters, rescue dogs and to contact law enforcement agencies and other government officials. An Accident Site Commander or Field Rescue Leader takes charge of the practical part of the rescue at the accident site. Other persons are designated to lead groups of rescuers to the site quickly and safely, to issue equipment to rescue groups and to keep track of everyone involved in the rescue.

A rescue plan usually consists of three stages. The first stage objective is to get the first party to the scene as quickly as possible and to conduct a hasty search in the hope of recovering the victim alive. The group will be lightly equipped with sectional probes, shovels, minimum first aid and some personal gear.

Stage two is a consolidation stage where a follow-up party is brought in along with sophisticated equipment for reviving the victim and ensuring his continued survival. In many cases the Accident Site Commander will travel with this group which, in a well organized rescue, will leave within a few minutes of the first stage but, because of toboggan loads of extra equipment, will travel more slowly.

Stage three is the support stage which may or may not be needed. In this stage food and hot drinks, extra clothing, more equipment, relief personnel and lighting, if required, will be transported to the site. In the case of a prolonged rescue a complete camp may be set up to allow rescuers to feed and rest between shifts.

A back-country rescue tends to produce three similar stages. The first is where the victim is located and dug out. The second consists of wrapping the victim up, applying first aid and seeing to the needs of the rescuers themselves. A third stage might involve keeping the victim alive overnight in a tent or snow cave.

Rescuing Another Party

There's always a chance that you'll see another party avalanched or be asked for help by the survivors.

If you're on the spot, note where the victim is when you first see him and watch him very carefully until the moment he disappears under the snow. Try to fix this last-seen area by some identifiable natural feature. As soon as you get onto the debris mark the area with a ski. If you haven't seen the accident, persuade the survivors to go back to the debris with you and describe exactly what happened, again marking the area where the victim was last-seen. Find out how many people were caught and if they had rescue beacons.

Fig. 10.4 The Richardson Ridge avalanche. X marks the approximate burial position. Photo by Kris Newman.

Rescuing a Member of Your Own Party

If you're aware of avalanche danger and are using proper slope crossing procedures you should have only one victim to worry about. Watch carefully as he's being carried down, noting what happens to skis, poles and other abandoned equipment. In particular fix your eyes on the area where the victim is last seen and send someone to mark the spot with a ski or some large identifiable object such as a pack. Consider the possibility of further avalanches.

The importance of watching the victim is well illustrated by an accident that happened near Lake Louise ski area in the Canadian Rockies. The first skier had left the top of Richardson's Ridge and was standing in a safe place below the slope watching the second skier come down. The second man, who'd chosen a slightly steeper line, had only made 10 turns when he triggered a slab avalanche which carried him down the slope and finally buried him. Because the first skier had been watching the whole sequence right up to the time when his friend disappeared, he was able to rush to the most likely area of debris and start probing with his probe pole. The fourth probe was successful. Fortunately he was carrying a shovel. In the few minutes it took to uncover the victims head he was unconscious, his airway plugged with snow. The rescuer said later *"We had no rescue beacons and were both lucky as hell."*

Doing the right thing helps too.

Fig. 10.5 Skiers rush to the aid of a buried
companion. The slide was triggered by another
skier crossing from right to left above the debris.
Photo by André Roch.

Search Without Rescue Beacons

— Ideally the most experienced member of the group should take charge.

— Check for danger from further avalanching especially in multi-branched gully systems and bowls which have only partially slid.

— Post a lookout to warn rescuers of further slides. Select an escape route known by all rescuers.

— Make a quick search of the debris for clues. Leave anything you find on the surface where it might serve to indicate the line taken by the victim.

— Using probes, or ski poles with the baskets removed, probe any likely areas around trees or rocks where the victim could have lodged.

— Glance up the runout zone to see if there is anywhere a person could have hung up on the way down.

— Most victims are found near the toe of the debris. Unless you have very good reason to suspect otherwise, concentrate on the last few metres of the debris.

— After all the likely locations have been probed, set up an organized probe line and probe the most likely areas of debris (usually the largest piles of debris in the main deposit close to the toe of the debris), marking with whatever you have available (skis, packs etc.) the areas as you probe them. Even if there are only two survivors, it is statistically more effective to probe in an organized manner.

— Keep the slide clean of food scraps, urine etc. in case a rescue dog has to be brought in.

Surface (Hasty) Search

The surface search is the most important part of a back-country rescue because it offers the greatest possibility of a live recovery.

There are several cases of partially buried victims having died because their companions didn't stop to search before going for help.

An accident report in The Avalanche Review stated that: *"... two backcountry skiers were caught in a slide near Aspen, Colorado. The survivor dug herself out, made a fast check of the debris and left the site to notify rescuers. Hours later, a hasty search by the rescue team revealed a ski tip sticking from the snow. The victim, shallowly buried, had died."*

Fig. 10.6 Victims of avalanche accidents may be injured by the twisting force of the snow intensified by the leverage of skis and poles. Photo by Bob Sandford, courtesy of Alberta Mountain Council.

Fig. 10.7 Use any item at your disposal when probing. The important rule is to probe in an organized manner. Photo by Bob Sandford, courtesy Alberta Mountain Council.

Probing

Probing is the oldest and least efficient method of searching for an avalanche victim. Unfortunately, if the victim and searchers are not equipped with avalanche rescue beacons it's the only method available to the back-country traveller. If correct probing techniques are used, there's a 70% chance of finding the victim on the first pass providing he's not buried too deeply. You'll probably be using ski poles which only allow you to probe to a depth of about 1.5 metres. The advantage of probe poles which extend to 3 metres is obvious.

There are two methods using probes to locate a buried person: coarse probing and fine probing. Coarse probing should be used when there's a chance of a live recovery; fine probing is a body recovery technique used by organized rescue groups. Because fine probing takes 4 or 5 times longer to complete it's more efficient to cover the ground several times using coarse probing.

To be effective, **probing must be organized and orderly**. Establish a leader to co-ordinate probing; usually the most experienced member of the party. The procedure for coarse probing is as follows:

— Probe uphill; this way it's easier to keep the proper spacing between probers. **Start from the very toe of the debris.**

— Estimate the line the victim might have taken using the last seen area and any articles found on the surface as clues. Probe up this line first, marking the boundaries of the area probed with skis.

— To get the proper spacing probers should stand, hand on hips, elbow to elbow. Keeping this spacing, each prober inserts the probe once between the feet.

— An alternative is to stand fingertip to fingertip and probe first to one side of your body and then to the other side. Use this method when there's a limited number of probers.

— After each probe the line moves forward about 2 boot lengths or one step and probes again. This procedure is repeated as far as necessary up the slope.

— The leader should to call out "probes up - forward - down" at which commands the probers should raise their probes, advance and probe down again. The manoeuvre must be done with military precision and to a rhythm which ensures maximum pace.

— The prober who hits a victim within 1.5 m of the surface will have no doubt about the contact. A tree stump or a rock feels much different.

— Dig out the victim. If you know or suspect there are other skiers buried under the debris, designate one or two people to dig out the first victim while the rest continue to probe.

— If you're unsuccessful on the first pass you must decide whether to probe the same area again or whether to move to an adjacent area. Unless you're absolutely sure that you're probing the right area you should move the probe line each time until you have covered all possibilities.

Fig. 10.8 The probe line for the search for the fourth Irishman on Ben Nevis, Scotland. See page 89 for an account of the accident. Photo by Andy Nicol.

Searching with Avalanche Rescue Beacons

An avalanche rescue beacon search is conducted in three phases: the signal from the victim's beacon is picked up, the area of burial is then located and finally the exact location of the victim is pinpointed.

Contrary to popular belief, rescue beacons are not direction finders. However, they do contain antennae and will pick up the signal more clearly when the two antennae are parallel. Although the position of the antenna in the buried unit isn't known you can orient your rescue beacon by turning it around and moving it up and down through 90 until the volume of the signal is loudest.

Initial Search for a Signal

Everyone must switch their rescue beacon to receive and make sure they're receiving at full volume if their unit has a volume control.

If there's any chance of further danger post a lookout and instruct everyone to switch to transmit should another avalanche occur.

Spread the party evenly across the slope at intervals of not more than 30 m. It doesn't matter if you search uphill, downhill or across the debris, as long as you walk in straight lines parallel to one another. If you're the only searcher zig-zag across the debris.

The whole party should stop every 15 to 20 paces and listen carefully, orienting the unit for optimum antenna direction. The advantage of stopping to listen is very apparent when searching on cold, crunchy snow. Apart from the occasional command the search should be conducted in silence.

Fig. 10.9 this photograph illustrates the two methods of searching avalanche debris to locate a signal. A large avalanche on the Oberalp, Gotthard, Switzerland. Photo by André Roch.

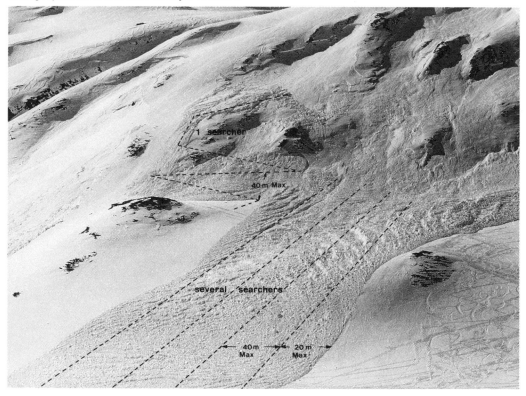

When a signal is picked up, assign one or two persons to track it down, while the rest of the group continues to search for other signals. If only one person is known to be caught, or when all the signals have been located, assign no more than two people to track down each signal. The remainder of the search party should be getting shovels and probes ready for the digging out.

Although you are searching for a victim known to have a rescue beacon, you should still mark the last seen area and entry point just in case the beacon was not switched to transmit at the time of the accident. Treat the initial rescue beacon search as part of the hasty search of the debris and mark all pertinent points.

Generally, searchers should wear their packs to ensure that rescue gear is close at hand. Keep ski poles handy in case they're needed as probes or as markers to delineate final search limits. You should take your skis off as soon as you reach the debris unless the snow is very soft. Usually it isn't.

Locating the Area of Burial

The "Grid" and "Induction Lines" search methods are described here. Try them both, and use the method which you find easiest and quickest.

There are variations possible with both methods. It is possible, with practice, to simplify and speed up the Grid search. The Ramer AvaLRT uses a variation of the Induction Lines method using both an audio and a visual "Range Alarm" signal.

Grid search When a signal's been picked up, the persons assigned to do the detailed search should keep going in the same straight line, making sure the beacon is oriented for maximum signal. As the volume increases turn the volume control down until you can just hear the signal. Refer to point "A" on Fig. 10.10.

Keep walking along the same line until the signal fades at "B". Mark this point with a ski pole or glove.

Keeping the beacon oriented the same way as before, turn through 180 and walk back along the same line, but don't change the volume this time. The signal will increase in volume then fade away again. Mark the point where the signal fades at "C", then backtrack to the middle of the two marked points "B" and "C" at "D".

At "D" turn 90° and listen carefully to the signal, orient the beacon again to achieve maximum volume. Turn the volume control down until you can only just hear the signal. Now walk at right angles to the original line, adjusting the volume control down as far as possible, until the signal fades at "E". Then turn 180° and walk back along the same line until the signal fades at "F". When you return to the middle at "G" you should be close to the buried person.

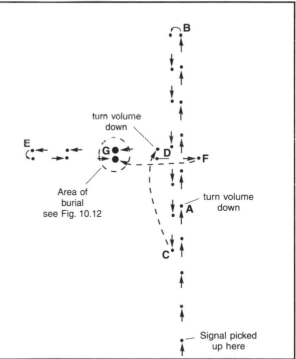

Fig. 10.10 The Grid search method for locating the area of burial. See text for description.

The "Induction Lines" Method

Once having picked up the signal during the initial search, hold the beacon horizontally with the top end (the Ortovox has a direction arrow) pointing forward. Turn yourself around until the signal is a maximum.

Walk forward in the direction the beacon is pointing for about 5 m, and stop (if the signal gets weaker, go in the opposite direction).

Realign the beacon for maximum signal, turning the volume down when possible, and walk forward for another 5 m. Except in rare cases where the antenna are exactly aligned, you should be walking in a curve along the induction line towards the victim.

When the signal is loudest at minimum volume you will be close to the victim and can begin to pinpoint the actual position.

Very short search times can be achieved, with practice, using this method.

Pinpointing the Position

Now you are very close, orient the unit for maximum signal again and sweep the beacon just above the surface of the snow in a criss-cross pattern. Find the location halfway between the points where the signal fades away. Trying to identify the point where the signal is strongest works well with some beacons. Usually you can locate a buried unit to an accuracy of about one third of the depth of burial. For instance, if the buried unit is 1 m deep then you should be able to locate the position within 1/3 m horizontally. Metal objects will deflect or reflect the signal, so keep skis, poles or shovels away from the burial location until you've finished the search.

Time can be saved by locating the exact position of the victim with a probe or ski pole before starting to dig. If another person is still buried turn off the found victim's beacon as soon as possible.

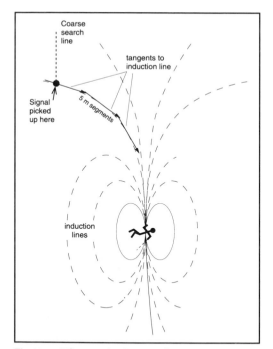

Fig. 10.11 When conducting an Induction Line search, the searcher walks in 5 m segments. At the end of each straight segment, the beacon is re-oriented for maximum signal.

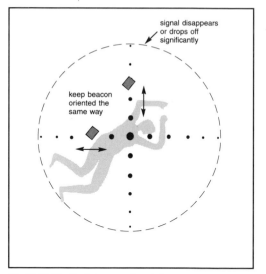

Fig. 10.12 The final stage — pinpointing the victim's location.

174

Sending for Help

Before sending for help, make quite sure that help is required. The leader should gather the group together and discuss with them exactly what kind of help is needed. A problem which plagues rescue organizations is a panic call before the circumstances and consequences of the accident have been determined. Start compiling a log of events and times.

Ideally, the request for help should be in writing; the message may then be passed on by laymen who might otherwise misinterpret terms used by the survivor; it's surprising how quickly and easily a message can become garbled. If possible send 2 people out for help. To respond effectively, rescue groups need answers to the following questions:

— Where did the accident take place and at what time.

— What travel conditions are like in the area and an estimate of how long it will take rescuers to reach them.

Fig. 10.13 The final stage in locating a buried avalanche beacon.

— Exactly what happened.

— How many persons are buried or injured?

— What are their injuries? Will they need special care?

— Some idea of the number of rescuers at the site, their experience and how well they are equipped.

— What help you expect of the rescuers.

— Any other information which might help in planning the rescue such as available helicopter landing sites, snow conditions, elevation of the accident site, weather — especially the amount of cloud, approximate temperature, and wind strength.

If You are Sent for Help

Your prime objective is to get help for injured or buried avalanche victims as quickly and as safely as possible. If you take too many chances and are injured on the way out, not only do you let your friends down but you also compound eventual rescue problems. So take it easy, relatively speaking, and try to arrive at your destination able to describe the accident in a calm and coherent manner.

In National Parks or other formally administered areas such as National Forests and Provincial Parks contact the Wardens or Park Rangers. In other areas call the closest Law Enforcement Agency who will get in touch with the appropriate rescue groups.

It's very important that having given your information you don't disappear. If you phone in the alarm give the number you are calling from and stay by the phone until you're contacted; usually the rescue leader will want to talk to you personally. If you're a sole survivor — the only eye witness — you'll have to return to the scene of the accident with the rescue group.

The Role of Helicopters in Rescue

— For a helicopter to come in at all requires reasonable visibility. They are highly susceptible to turbulence and high ground winds

— They can't hover over dense brush, or over slopes of more than 10°, but can rest for short periods on one skid.

— Few helicopters can land or take off vertically; they require additional space for a short landing or take-off run.

— Pilots need a visual reference to pinpoint the snow surface. Skis, lying flat at the side of a packed down area work well. Don't use light weight items such as jackets or foamies. Don't stand skis up in the snow anywhere near the landing site.

— When a helicopter is coming in to land, indicate wind direction by standing with your back to the wind and your arms outstretched in front of you pointing to the landing site.

— Don't leave loose items near a landing site; they're liable to be sucked up into the main or tail rotor causing damage which will immobilize the machine.

Fig. 10.14 Skiers and climbers should be familiar with a helicopter's limitations and know how to behave safely around a helicopter. Photo by Bob Sandford, courtesy Alberta Mountain Council.

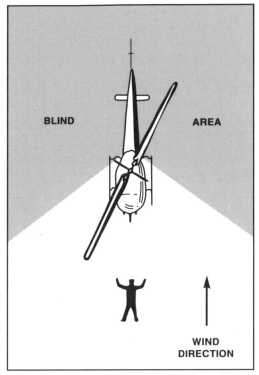

Fig. 10.15 When approaching a helicopter remain within the pilot's field of view.

Staying Alive around a helicopter

— The most important rule. **Don't panic**

— Stay where you can be seen by the pilot.

— **Never** go around the back of a helicopter. Wait for the pilot's signal before approaching. If the landing site has a slight slope to it remember that rotor clearance on the uphill side is reduced.

— Beware of the main rotor, tail rotor, exhaust pipes and air intakes. Avoid touching protuberances at the front which may either be delicate or hot.

— Never carry equipment above shoulder height when approaching or leaving a helicopter.

Avalanche Rescue Summary

Establish a leader. Usually the most experienced member of the group will take charge.

Assess the chance of further avalanche danger. If necessary have someone keep watch and advise all rescuers of the escape route.

Do not send for help immediately unless help is very close.

Mark the spot where the victim was last seen with a ski or ski pole .

Quickly examine debris for signs of the victim or his equipment. Dig out partially buried poles or skis; they could be attached to the victim. If the accident involves another party find out how many are buried. Do they have avalanche rescue beacons? If so start a beacon search.

Probe likely spots in the main deposit and behind trees or rocks using ski poles with baskets ripped off. If you watched the accident, probe briefly in the area where you think the victim ended up. Check for persons hung up in trees or behind rocks in the runout zone.

Organize a probe line. After the first brief search, organized probing is preferable to random probing. Get in a line, spaced hands on hips, elbow to elbow and probe likely areas. Work uphill.

Send 2 people for help if you haven't found the victim in the first hour. After one hour the chance for survival is down to about 30%.

Continue probing as long as there is hope. Cover all areas where slide debris has accumulated. Mark areas as they are probed and clues as they are dug up.

Look after the rescuers. Make sure they don't become casualties of exhaustion and hypothermia.

Avalanche Rescue Dogs

An avalanche rescue dog's air scenting ability is a very efficient method of finding buried victims. In Europe between the years of 1962 and 1972 dogs participated in 135 rescues and were responsible for the live recovery of 25 people. The picture in North America is a little different: to date there have only been three or four live rescues of skiers and climbers in the backcountry. Because fewer dogs are spread out over a very much larger area, the time spent in getting them to the scene of the accident means less chance of finding the victim alive.

In April 1992, a skier skiing just outside the Jackson Hole ski area boundary took a 300 m ride over 2 cliff bands and was buried over a metre deep. An air pocket kept him alive until found by a rescue dog after being buried for 1 hour 33 minutes. Ten years earlier, a ski lift operator at Alpine Meadows (California) was found after five days of burial in the wreckage of the summit terminal building.

In reasonable weather conditions, a dog will find all victims who are still alive and those who have just died regardless of the depth or nature of the snow. If the body has been dead some time and is frozen a dog will only be effective to a depth of around 2 metres in porous snow, which is further reduced to a metre or less in hard compact snow.

There are a few things a rescue party should do which will help a dog:

— Keep probe lines going until instructed to do otherwise by the dogmaster. Sometimes the dog can work an area at the same time as a probe line. On no account stop searching and wait for the dog to arrive.

— Avoid contaminating the debris with food scraps, candy wrappers, urine, cigarette butts, etc. If you get the chance, move packs and other surplus equipment off and downwind of the debris

Fig 10.16 Dogmaster Chris Banham works "Attila" during a practice session. Photo by Greg Crawford, courtesy Peter Lougheed Provincial Park.

11

Avalanche First Aid

After an accident there's always a considerable amount of excitement, anxiety and sometimes numbing fear on the part of the rescuers especially if friends or loved ones are involved. Having a definite procedure to follow helps restore calm and gives the victim the best chance of recovery.

Uncovering the Victim

Your first objective is to uncover the head, clear obstructions around the mouth and nose and free the chest and abdomen from constriction as soon as possible. Be very careful not to cut the victim with the shovel during the final stages of freeing the head and body.

When the depth of burial is more than one metre, it is more efficient to start digging downhill or to one side of the victim and angle in; this way, it's easier to get rid of surplus snow. While you're doing this, mentally rehearse what you will do when the victim is uncovered. Preferably, if there's enough help around, let others do the digging and just stand aside for a few minutes and think; it may result in fewer mistakes or serious omissions later on.

Deal with Life-threatening Emergencies First

As soon as the victim's head is uncovered, look for a plug of snow in or around the mouth and nose. Removal may lead to spontaneous breathing.

If the Victim is not Breathing

After making sure the airway isn't blocked, examine the neck quickly by running the fingers firmly down the upper part of the spine from the base of the skull to the shoulder blades. Feel for any obvious deformity. Sometimes an involuntary reflex movement indicates a neck injury even though the patient is unconscious.

Check for pulse; the carotid artery in the neck is the most obvious place. Try for at least 10 seconds or longer if the victim has been buried for any length of time. If you cannot identify a pulse don't assume that the victim is dead; a faint pulse is very hard to detect in an accident situation. Look for other indications that the heart has stopped beating such as cyanosis (a blue-gray appearance of areas of the skin which are normally pink like finger nails and lips) and dilation of the pupils coupled with lack of reaction to light.

Don't give up hope at this stage, particularly if the victim was found with an air pocket in front of their face. Start artificial respiration at once using the mouth to mouth resuscitation method. It's been found that warmed air blown into the victim's lungs is of more benefit than cold air forced in by other resuscitation methods.

If a neck injury is suspected, the head should be moved as little as possible and the airway opened by placing your hands on either side of the head to maintain the neck in a fixed, neutral position while at the same time pushing the jaw forward with the index fingers. Ideally two persons are needed for this method, although one person can do it at a pinch by sealing the nose using their cheek — but it's a difficult and tiring job.

If you cannot find a pulse and have been trained in Cardiopulmonary Resuscitation techniques then by all means apply them. But first, move the victim very gently to a firm surface. In such cases great care must be taken to ensure that there's no pulse before CPR is started.

Continue resuscitation for at least 2 hours making sure during this time that the patient is protected from further cooling. Treat for severe bleeding if necessary.

Identify Other Injuries

Once the victim is breathing make a complete body survey. Check pupils for irregularity and response, look for obvious face and head injuries, re-check the neck and back, run fingers across the collarbone and squeeze the pelvis at the hips. Look for less serious injuries to arms and legs. Unless you have a definite indication of chest and abdomen injuries, it's best under the circumstances to leave the patient covered-up.

Removing the Victim

It doesn't matter whether a victim is conscious or unconscious, they must be removed from the snow gently. It's possible they're suffering from hypothermia to some degree, especially if they have been buried for some time, and a cold heart is very vulnerable to shaking or jarring; in severe cases there's the danger of death from ventricular fibrillation. While moving the victim to a safe place stop and check pulse and breathing every few minutes.

When you reach shelter, the unconscious person should be placed in a semi-prone position with the head level and slightly lower than the body. The airway must be kept open.

Keeping the Patient Alive

If the victim is still unconscious, monitor their vital signs constantly. You should note the level of consciousness, pupil size and reaction, respiration rate (14 to 18 cycles per minute is normal) and pulse rate (60 to 90 per minute is normal). Any anomalies should be written down and conveyed to the hospital with the patient.

Maintain the victim's body heat right from the time the patient is uncovered until professional help arrives. Because an injured person is likely to be partially or totally immobilized they're very much more susceptible to frostbite and hypothermia than the rescuers who can exercise to keep warm. Cold coupled with pain and worry about their injuries can bring on shock.

Shock and Hypothermia

Fortunately, the treatment for shock and hypothermia in a rescue situation is identical. First of all get the patient into shelter, whether a tent, snow cave or trench in the ground. Remove boots and socks, either replacing wet socks with dry ones or wrapping the feet in a dry wool sweater.

The feet and lower legs should be elevated and placed inside a packsack. Withdraw the arms from the sleeves of his jacket and sweater and arrange inside the clothing against the trunk. Cover the head. Wrap the person further in any material which will help conserve body heat such as a space blanket or polythene tube tent. If the patient is very cold — slipping into a hypothermic condition — get one of the rescuers to strip off to his underwear and wrap them up together using their outer clothing and a space blanket. A sleeping bag makes this technique much easier to implement. If you have the means to heat water you can make a hot compress. Soak a shirt or other article of clothing in very hot water, put it in a plastic bag and wrap the whole thing in a sweater. Place the compress on the patient's abdomen just below the sternum, binding it to the patient with spare clothing. If you have the facilities, in a hut for instance, additional compresses can be used against the side of the chest immediately below the arms. Don't massage the victims arms or legs as this encourages cold blood to flow from the extremities to the body core.

If the victim is fully conscious give hot, preferably non-sweetened drinks. Do not give alcohol. Handle gently to avoid any jarring or bouncing which might lead to ventricular fibrillation.

Frostbite

Keeping the patient warm helps prevent frostbite. However, injured extremities, especially if splinted, are extremely prone to frostbite and frequent inspection is necessary to make sure there's adequate circulation. If you have to stay near the accident scene overnight, thaw out frozen extremities using body heat or warm water providing you can keep them from re-freezing. Do not allow a person to walk or ski once their feet have been thawed out.

Pain

Because pain contributes to the development of shock, a patient who asks for relief should be given it. Two tablets every 3 hours of 50 mg Demerol or 30 mg Codeine are sufficient for most situations. A relaxant such as Vallium is useful in calming down the patient and reducing excessive muscular spasms. A word of warning: do not give drugs if a patient is hypothermic; this includes subcutaneous or intramuscular injections which initially remain in the periphery, only entering the circulatory system in uncontrolled doses after successful rewarming.

Psychological Care

When a person is injured, the accompanying emotional shock can have a great influence on the outcome of the accident. In a back-country accident there's the additional worry of being far from qualified help and the likelihood of having to survive for a long time in an unfriendly environment.

The accident victim has two immediate psychological problems. First, there's a loss of self esteem at having been involved in an accident; the realization that they have done something stupid is further aggravated by the fact that they're now dependent on someone else's skill in order to survive. Second, they have very real fears concerning the extent of their injuries and the quality of care they're going to get. Because an injured person is so wrapped up in their own immediate survival, they becomes prone to making irrational decisions and voicing seemingly irrelevant concerns.

Rescuers must try to restore a persons dignity. Let the patient discuss the accident, but be careful not to moralize or pass judgement at this stage. If you don't know the victim find out their first name and use it frequently when speaking to them. Involve them in their own care by giving them something useful to do. Above all try not to give any indication that they are a burden on the rescue party.

It is reassuring to an avalanche victim if the rescue, particularly the first aid, is conducted in a calm orderly manner. Introduce yourself to the patient and give them some indication of your qualifications: the number of years you've been mountaineering or skiing, your first aid training and rescue experience. Find out the patients name and home town and if they have any medical problems which might affect treatment such as diabetes or drug allergy. Give them an honest appraisal of their injuries, then discuss treatment, explaining as you go along what you are doing and why. Someone should sit by their side at all times.

Evacuation

At some time during the rescue you'll have to make a decision on how the victim is to be evacuated. There are three reasonable alternatives:

— The rescue party can evacuate the victim themselves before or shortly after nightfall.

— A rescue organization capable of reaching the accident scene before dark can be called in.

— Evacuation cannot be started until the next day and the group has to survive overnight.

Self Evacuation

If the victim is merely shaken up or only slightly injured they will probably prefer to get out without calling in a rescue group and should be encouraged to do so. Bear in mind that skis are often lost in the accident and walking a long distance in deep snow is exhausting and conducive to frostbite. Don't allow a person who has been unconscious or who has developed hypothermia to walk out, even if they say that they feel capable.

Another alternative is to build an improvised toboggan from skis and poles; instructions are given in most texts on winter survival or ski touring. The main function of an improvised toboggan is to transport an injured person a short distance to a place of safety. Long hauls with makeshift equipment in any but the easiest terrain and the best snow conditions require a tremendous amount of manpower and in deep, fresh snow can quickly exhaust a rescue party thereby jeopardizing the entire operation. Moreover, moving a badly injured person in this manner can greatly aggravate any injuries and add substantially to the effects of shock. Often it's far better to spend precious time and energy building a survival shelter and to concentrate on keeping the patient alive and warm until professional help arrives.

Rescue Before Nightfall

In both Europe and North America organized rescue groups can speedily transport an injured person by helicopter, snowmobile or rescue toboggan to hospital. If it is obvious that such a group can effect a rescue before nightfall it's better to stay put near the scene of the accident and wait for help. Build windbreaks, light a fire, and if a helicopter is expected, stamp out a landing place in the nearest flat open area.

By now the rescuers are probably tired, cold and hungry. If it's feasible, send all those who are no longer needed out to the road. Those who stay can keep warm by skiing around or building extra shelters. Watch for signs of frostbite resulting from perspiration built up during the rescue. Now is the time to change socks, put on overboots and concentrate on your own survival.

Surviving Overnight

When an accident happens late in the day or at a remote location an overnight bivouac is a certainty. If there's enough time send as many people as you can afford back to camp or out to civilization.

For those remaining, getting out of the wind and putting some kind of insulating layer between yourselves and the cold air is the first priority. Move to the lee side of rocks or down to treeline. Look for a suitable place to construct a snow shelter. Circumstances will dictate how elaborate a shelter you construct; in really foul weather you may only have enough energy left to dig a shallow trench covered with snow blocks. More time, more energy and suitable snow would allow the construction of a snow cave or igloo. A small stove, even a candle, will raise the air temperature in a confined space close to freezing point.

First Aid Summary

Uncovering the victim. Uncover the head and clear obstructions around the mouth and nose. Free the chest and abdomen from constriction. Think about what first aid may be required.

Deal with life threatening emergencies first. Clear the airway and restore breathing. Stop severe bleeding. Prevent further cooling.

Identify other injuries. Make a complete body survey. Plan and carry out treatment.

Removing the victim. Remove gently — treat as though hypothermic. Be particularly careful with victims who have suffered neck or back injuries.

Keeping the patient alive. Treat for shock and hypothermia. Be aware of the potential for frostbite. Treat for pain. Reassure the patient.

Evacuation. Decide whether or not you can get the victim out before nightfall. Does a rescue group need to be called in? If help isn't likely to arrive before the next day, think about surviving overnight.

Surviving overnight. If you don't have tents make a shelter to get you out of the wind. If time allows construct a snow cave or igloo.

Bibliography

American Alpine Club & Alpine Club of Canada, **"Accidents in North American Mountaineering"**, New York & Banff, Published annually since 1948. (Synopsis of mountaineering accidents; often include avalanche accidents)

Armstrong, B and Williams, K., **"The Avalanche Book"**, Fulcrum, Inc., revised 1992, 232 p. (An informative book on avalanches and their impact on those who live, work or recreate in mountain areas.)

Atwater, M.M., **"The Avalanche Hunters"**, MacRae Smith Co., Philadelphia, 1968, 236 p. Out of print. (Autobiography describing avalanche studies and the development of control procedures in the U.S.A.)

Barton, B. and Wright, B., **"A Chance in a Million?"**, The Scottish Mountaineering Trust, 1985, 120 p. (Avalanche safety handbook for Scotland)

Bentley, W.A. & Humphreys, W.J., **"Snow Crystals"**, Dover Publications Inc., New York, 1962, 226 p. (2453 illustrations of snow crystals)

Bryson, S., **"Search and Rescue Dog Training"**, Boxwood Press, CA., 1976, 212 p.

Diltz-Siler, B., **"Understanding Avalanches"**, Signpost Publications, Lynnwood, WA., 1977, 32 p. (A handbook for snow travellers in the Sierras and Cascades)

Fraser, C., **"Avalanches and Snow Safety"**, John Murray, London, 1978, 269 p. Former edition titled The Avalanche Enigma. (A non-technical account of snow and avalanches based on the author's experiences in the Swiss Alps)

Fredston, J.A. and Fesler, D., **"Snow Sense - A Guide to Evaluating Avalanche Hazard"**, Alaska Mountain Safety Centre, Inc. 1988, 48 p. (Small pocket book for backcountry travellers)

Girardi, W. ed. **"Lawinen Handbuch"**, Tyrolia-Verlag Innsbruck - Wien, c. 1987, 224 p. (A German language equivalent of The Avalanche Handbook).

LaChapelle, E.R., **"A.B.C. of Avalanche Safety"**, Mountaineers, Seattle, 1985, 112 p. (Small pocket book giving basics of avalanche safety and rescue)

LaChapelle, E.R., **"Field Guide to Snow Crystals"**, University of Washington Press, 1969, 101 p. (Snow metamorphism with illustrations of snow crystals)

Perla, R.I., **"Snow Crystals/Les cristaux de neige"**, NHRI Paper No 1, National Hydrology Research Institute, Ottawa, 1978, 19 p. (Descriptions and illustrations of the various types of crystals in the snowpack)

Perla, R.I. & Martinelli, M. Jr., **"Avalanche Handbook"**, Agriculture Handbook 489, U.S. Government Printing Office, Washington, D.C., revised ed. 1978, 254 p. (A technical handbook for those engaged in avalanche control and forecasting)

Seligman, G., **"Snow Structures and Ski Fields"**, International Glaciological Society, Cambridge, England, 1980, 555 p. (Third edition of the book first published in 1936. Although dated is a good introduction to the subject of snow and avalanches.)

Valla, F., **"Ski et Securite"**, Glénat and Association Nationale pour L'etude de la Neige et des Avalanches, 1991, 130 p. (French language book on avalanche safety)

Glossary

Accumulation Zone An area where snow accumulates either by direct deposition or by wind transport. In avalanche terminology it usually refers to the starting zone.

Avalanche Defined in dictionaries as a mass of snow, rock and ice falling down a mountain. In practice the term avalanche refers to the snow avalanche unless the words rock, ice mud etc. are specifically used. In the U.S. the term snowslide is commonly used to mean a snow avalanche.

Aspect The compass direction of a slope looking straight down the fall line.

Bed Surface The surface on which a slab avalanche slides. If only the top layers of the snow slide off an underlying snow layer the avalanche is described as a surface avalanche. If the entire snow cover slides off to the ground it is called a full-depth avalanche.

Channelled Avalanche An avalanche which is confined by flutings or by a gully as opposed to an avalanche on an open slope which is referred to as Unconfined.

Climax Avalanche Many people consider any large and devastating avalanche to be a climax avalanche but this is not correct. A Climax Avalanche is the culmination of the build-up of several layers on top of a weak one. Large climax avalanches occur in spring when the whole of the seasons snowpack may release right down to the ground.

Corn Snow is composed of large granular snow grains resulting from many cycles of melting and re-freezing. Sometimes called Spring Snow, it gives fabulous skiing for a limited time period as it begins to melt — until the snow becomes so wet as to be slushy.

Creep Is an internal deformation of the snowpack reflecting the snow's ability to flow like a liquid, albeit very slowly.

Crown Fracture Line, Crown Line, Crown Surface all refer to the top fracture line of a slab avalanche.

Crust A hard, fairly thin layer formed of well-bonded snow. Bonding may be due to refreezing of melted grains (Sun Crust) or wind packing (Wind Crust).

Crystal A solid, whose atoms or molecules have a regularly repeated arrangement. In snow terminology there is some confusion between grain and crystal. Rounding causes a snow crystal to loose its crystalline structure and become a blob (grain) of ice. Faceting is the beginning of the recrystallization process where an orderly arrangement of water molecules begins to build up on a grain of ice. In some processes such a surface hoar, water molecules recrystallize to form new crystals.

Cup Crystal A hollow cup-shaped depth hoar crystal usually found hanging open end down in relatively large open spaces in the snowpack. A supply of moisture, very still air and a large temperature gradient are required for their formation. Large depth hoar crystals in the base of the snowpack are also called cup crystals. See also Sugar Snow.

Delayed-action Avalanches are avalanches which release at any time between storms without warning. Also called Non Storm-induced avalanches.

Deposition Zone The area where the bulk of the snow carried down in an avalanche comes to rest. See also Runout Zone and Windblast Zone.

Depth Hoar Recrystallized snow found in the bottom layers of a shallow snowpack after a period of very cold weather. Commonly called Sugar Snow.

Direct-action Avalanches are avalanches which fall during or shortly after a storm. Also called Storm-induced avalanches.

Equilibrium Form Used by the snow science community to describe the form of ice grain created by the rounding process. This form is the result of little or no crystal growth.

Equi-temperature Metamorphism A term formerly used to describe the process of rounding. See metamorphism.

Faceted Grains, or Angular Grains are grains with facets or faces separated by sharp corners. They're the beginning stage of recrystallization due to large temperature gradients.

Firn Snow Snow which has settled and compacted under the influence of both Melt-freeze and Pressure Metamorphism. Common usage considers firn snow to be snow which has survived the spring thaw.

Flank Surface The fracture lines at the sides of a slab avalanche. The left flank is the left fracture line as you look downhill in the direction of fall.

Fracture Line The division between the sliding slab and the stable snow above and to each side. See Crown Fracture Line and Flank Surface.

Full-Depth Avalanches are avalanches which clean off the snow right down to the ground.

Funicular Regime The condition, in wet snow, where the liquid content is high enough for the water to exits in a continuous path between grains, resulting in very weak bond.

Glide is the slow steady movement of a snow slab over either the ground surface or over a wetted layer within the snowpack such as ice.

Glide Crack The crack formed by the gliding of a slab. Such cracks tend to widen over a period of time and eventually the slab may fall as an avalanche.

Gliding Surface is the term sometimes used instead of Bed Surface when referring to the surface on which a slab avalanche slides. A weak layer above the gliding surface is known as the Slide Layer.

Grain A single particle of ice; the smallest individual component of snow on the ground. A distinction is usually made between Snow Crystals and Ice Grains. Snow crystals fall from the atmosphere and change into ice grains after they reach the ground. See Metamorphism. In some conditions of temperature and humidity, water vapor around ice grains may recrystallize to form ice crystals. See Surface Hoar and Depth Hoar.

Granular Snow Snow with relatively large grains or clusters of grains (>3 mm). Examples are large faceted surface grains, clusters of re-frozen melt-freeze grains, or heavily rimed snow crystals.

Graupel Atmospheric snow crystals heavily coating with rime before deposition.

Hard Slab Commonly used for slab which forms at higher altitudes with strong winds. Breaks up on release into large blocks which remain intact in the debris. There is no definable division between soft and hard slabs.

Ice Ice grains frozen together, with isolated pores and a density greater than about 830 kg/m^3

Ice Grain See Grain

Ice Lens Formed when free water percolates into a cold region of the snowpack and re-freezes.

Indicator Slope Slopes which tend to be the first to release avalanches after a storm are often referred to as Indicator Slopes; they indicate to the observer that snow stability is reaching a critical stage.

Isothermal Slides are wet snow avalanches which occur as a result of the top layers, or even the whole snowpack, attaining the same temperature throughout. In avalanche terminology the temperature referred to is a temperature close to O°C.

Kinetic Growth Form Used by the snow science community to describe the process of recrystallization causing faceting and the formation of cup-shaped crystals, and which is the result of rapid crystal growth.

Loose Snow Avalanches are avalanches which start from a point and gather more snow as they descend.

Lubricating Layer Normally used to describe a layer within the snowpack which has been wetted by free water percolating through the snow. Sometimes, any weak or cohesionless layer, such as a layer of buried surface hoar, is called a lubricating layer.

Melt-freeze See Metamorphism.

Metamorphism means change of form and is the name given to changes in the structure of the snow within the snowpack. The snow science community have made several changes in terminology during the last 30 years.

The terms currently used are: "Equilibrium Form" (rounding), "Kinetic Growth Form" (faceting or recrystallization), "Melt Freeze" and "Pressure metamorphism".

The old terms Equi-temperature and Temperature Gradient Metamorphism, Constructive and Destructive Metamorphism are no longer used in North America.

Necks are narrow connections between grains which give strength to the snowpack. They are formed by a migration of water molecules from the rounded portion of the grain to the concavity formed where grains come into contact. See Sintering.

New Snow The surface layer of snow as it is deposited and for some time after deposition.

Partially Settled Snow New snow which has undergone some rounding. It is usually stronger than new snow and has settled somewhat.

Pellet Snow Another name for graupel.

Pendular Regime The condition of snow with low liquid-water content where air exists in continuous paths and grain-to-grain bonds give strength to the snow layer.

Pore Spaces are the spaces within the snowpack between grains. In normal density snow they interconnect so that water or water vapor can flow through. In high density snow they can be non-communicating and therefore impervious to water vapor.

Powder Snow Avalanches are avalanches in which the snow breaks up into dust and may become airborne. Generally they're not influenced by obstacles in their path and can flow in a straight line over irregular terrain.

Pressure Metamorphism Metamorphism due to the weight of additional snow layers on the snowpack. The end product of pressure metamorphism, if the snow does not melt, is glacier ice.

Recrystallization The process of water vapor subliming onto an ice surface to form a structured ice crystal. Surface hoar and depth hoar are two examples.

Runout Zone The portion of the avalanche path where snow slows down and comes to rest. The area where the bulk of the snow piles up is called the Deposition Zone.

Rutschblock A column of snow, about 2 m square, excavated from the snowpack. The block is loaded by a skier, on skis. The point in the loading cycle at which it fails in shear is an indication of the snow stability at that location.

Settlement The process by which the snowpack becomes denser. In old snow layers settlement takes place at a rate of about 1 cm per day. New snow layers have much faster rates of settlement. The amount and speed of settlement is an indication of the strengthening of the snow layers.

Sintering The joining together of ice grains by the formation of necks between adjacent grains.

Slab Avalanches are avalanches which start when a large area of cohesive snow begins to slide at the same time.

Slope Angle The angle of incline of a slope measured from the horizontal.

Sluffs are small snow slides running less than 50 metres; small enough to be considered harmless to people.

Snow Cover see Snowpack.

Snow Crystal Usually reserved for snow formed by vapor deposition in the atmosphere. Crystals formed in a similar way on the ground are called Ice Crystals. The difference between Snow Crystals and Ice Grains is apparent when viewed through a magnifying glass.

Snow Cushion A smooth rounded deposit of soft slab formed on a lee slope. The slab under a cornice is a good example.

Snowslide see Avalanche.

Snowpack The combined layers of snow on the ground at any one time. Also called the Snow Cover. The snowpack is bounded by the Snow Surface and the Ground Surface.

Soft Slab Slab which loses its cohesion on release and breaks up into relatively small pieces.

Starting Zone The area where unstable snow breaks loose from the snowcover and starts to slide. It's the most dangerous area of the avalanche path for the climber and skier.

Stauchwall The line where the snow released in a slab avalanche rides up over the stable snow below. There is no English translation for this German word.

Sublimation is the ability of a substance to change from solid to vapor and back again without passing through the liquid stage. Common substances able to sublime are water and iodine.

Sugar Snow see Depth Hoar.

Surface Avalanches are avalanches which only involve the top layers of the snow and which slide on an underlying snow layer.

Temperature Gradient The difference in temperature through a given depth of snow. Expressed in Degrees Celsius per metre of snow. For example 10°C/m.

Temperature-gradient metamorphism The former name given to the process of recrystallization. Now referred to as faceting or recrystallization, the process results in the Kinetic Growth Form of ice crystals.

Terrain Trap Small terrain features which hold enough snow to bury a person. They're usually places which inexperienced people would not consider to be dangerous.

Track The slope or channel down which snow moves at a more or less uniform speed.

Trigger An Avalanche Trigger is the force which starts the snow sliding. It may be a Natural trigger such as the weight of additional snowfall or an Artificial trigger; such as the weight of a skier crossing the slope.

Unconfined Avalanches are avalanches which occur on open slopes.

Windblast Zone The area of the runout zone where airborne snow dust is deposited. In very large airborne avalanches an Airblast Zone may be present around both the track and the runout zone.

Selected References

"Avalanche Notes", U.S.Forest Service Westwide Avalanche Network, Rocky Mountain Forest & Range Experimental Station.

"The Snowy Torrents - Avalanche Accidents in the United States 1910 to 1966". Editor Dale Gallagher. U.S. Forest Service 1967.

"The Snowy Torrents - Avalanche Accidents in the United States 1967 to 1971". Editor Knox Williams. U.S. Forest Service 1975.

"Avalanche Accidents in Canada 1. A Selection of Case Histories of Accidents, 1955 to 1976". C.J.Stethem and P.A.Schaerer, National Research Council Division of Building Research Paper No.834, 1979.

"Avalanche Accidents in Canada 2. A Selection of Case Histories of Accidents, 1943 to 1978". C.J.Stethem and P.A.Schaerer, National Research Council Division of Building Research Paper No.926, 1980.

"Guidelines for Weather, Snowpack, and Avalanche Observations". National Research Council of Canada Technical Memorandum No. 132.

"Avalanche - Proceedings of a Symposium for Skiers, Ski-Mountaineers and Mountaineers, with accounts of experiences of Avalanches in Scotland, Europe and the Himalayas". J.Harding, M.Baker and E. Williams editors. Alpine Club, London, 1980.

"Avalanches - Protection, Location, Rescue". Vanni Eigenmann Foundation, 1979.

"The Avalanche Review". A publication of the American Association of Avalanche Professionals. Published monthly from November to April. P.O. Box 510904, Salt Lake City, Utah 84151-0904, USA

"The International Classification for Seasonal Snow on the Ground". The International Commission on Snow and Ice of the International Association of Scientific Hydrology along with the International Glaciological Society, 1990.

Index